THE BOOK OF LEGENDS
THE MAKING OF THE CHICKEN, LION, DRAGON HEART

by LINKED IN AND TOWN HALL ACHIEVER OF THE YEAR
EY NOMINEE ENTREPRENEUR OF THE YEAR
GRAND HOMAGE LYS DIVERSITY

Dr. BAK NGUYEN, DMD

&

by 8 year old

WILLIAM BAK

TO ALL THE LOVING PARENTS LOOKING TO CONNECT AND EDUCATE THEIR KIDS, HERE IS MY JOURNEY AND MY SECRETS.

by Dr. BAK NGUYEN
& WILLIAM BAK

Copyright © 2019 Dr. BAK NGUYEN

All rights reserved.

ISBN: 978-1-989536-27-8

THE BOOK OF LEGENDS
THE MAKING OF THE CHICKEN, LION, DRAGON HEART
by Dr. BAK NGUYEN & WILLIAM BAK

INTRODUCTION
BY Dr. BAK NGUYEN

ACT I
THE CHICKEN HEART

THE CHICKEN HEART
CHAPTER 1- Dr. BAK NGUYEN
A CHICKEN HEART NEEDS TO BE OPEN MINDED TO GROW

OPEN MIND
CHAPTER 2 - Dr. BAK NGUYEN & WILLIAM BAK
EAT TO GROW

FAMILY
HAPTER 3 - Dr. BAK NGUYEN & WILLIAM BAK
WHEN IT'S HARD IT'S TIME FOR ME TO LEARN

ACTION
CHAPTER 4 - Dr. BAK NGUYEN & WILLIAM BAK
DANCE TO BE HAPPY

TRUTH
CHAPTER 5 - Dr. BAK NGUYEN & WILLIAM BAK
TRUTH GOOD, LIE BAD

BE COOL
CHAPTER 6 - Dr. BAK NGUYEN & WILLIAM BAK
BE COOL TO BE SMOOTH

LOSING
CHAPTER 7 - Dr. BAK NGUYEN & WILLIAM BAK
NO LOSER, JUST LEARNER

DREAMS
CHAPTER 8 - Dr. BAK NGUYEN & WILLIAM BAK
THE COURAGE TO FOLLOW YOUR DREAMS

GROWTH
CHAPTER 9- Dr. BAK NGUYEN & WILLIAM BAK
LEARN, EAT AND GROW

STILL A CHICKEN
CHAPTER 10- Dr. BAK NGUYEN
SUPER CHICKEN

ACT II
THE LION HEART

THE LION HEART
CHAPTER 11 - Dr. BAK NGUYEN
I WAS STEEL. I KNEW FIRE. IT WAS TIME FOR ME TO COMBINE THE TWO OF THEM.
WILL AND LOVE.

FUN
CHAPTER 12- Dr. BAK NGUYEN & WILLIAM BAK
LEARN TO LAUGH

FEELING BETTER
CHAPTER 13- Dr. BAK NGUYEN & WILLIAM BAK
BEING GRATEFUL

GROWTH
CHAPTER 14- Dr. BAK NGUYEN & WILLIAM BAK
FIRST YOU NEED TO RELAX

LISTEN
CHAPTER 15 - Dr. BAK NGUYEN & WILLIAM BAK
TO TRY SOMETHING NEW

DARKNESS
CHAPTER 16 - Dr. BAK NGUYEN & WILLIAM BAK
BE CALM

SADNESS
CHAPTER 17 - Dr. BAK NGUYEN & WILLIAM BAK
A BIG HEART

ENJOY
CHAPTER 18 - Dr. BAK NGUYEN & WILLIAM BAK
ENJOY TODAY

FLY
CHAPTER 19- Dr. BAK NGUYEN & WILLIAM BAK
JUST THE BEGINNING

BLESSING
CHAPTER 20- Dr. BAK NGUYEN
GIVE AND YOU SHALL RECEIVE

ACT III
THE DRAGON HEART

THE DRAGON HEART
CHAPTER 21- Dr. BAK NGUYEN
LEARNING TO FLY

FLEX-I-BLE
CHAPTER 22- Dr. BAK NGUYEN & WILLIAM BAK
CHANGING SHAPE

THE POWER
CHAPTER 23- Dr. BAK NGUYEN & WILLIAM BAK
STAY IN CONTROL

FEAR
CHAPTER 24 - Dr. BAK NGUYEN & WILLIAM BAK
FEAR WILL DISAPPEAR WITH ACTION

EMOTIONS
CHAPTER 25 - Dr. BAK NGUYEN & WILLIAM BAK
HOW MANY DRAGONS ARE OUT THERE?

TRANSCENDENCE
CHAPTER 26 - Dr. BAK NGUYEN & WILLIAM BAK
FROM SADNESS WILL COME JOY

SECRET
CHAPTER 27 - Dr. BAK NGUYEN & WILLIAM BAK
THE CHICKEN BRAIN

FORCE OF NATURE
CHAPTER 28 - Dr. BAK NGUYEN & WILLIAM BAK
DRAGONS DON'T FIGHT AMONG THEMSELVES

FOREVER
CHAPTER 29 - Dr. BAK NGUYEN & WILLIAM BAK
THE CIRCLE OF THE DRAGON

FOREVER YOUNG
CHAPTER 30 - Dr. BAK NGUYEN & WILLIAM BAK
... JUST LIKE AT THE BEGINNING...

EASE & FLUIDITY
CHAPTER 31 - Dr. BAK NGUYEN
THE DRAGON'S JOURNEY

ACT IV
WE ARE ALL DRAGONS

WE ARE ALL DRAGONS
CHAPTER 32 - Dr. BAK NGUYEN
INFINITY

THE SHARK
CHAPTER 33- Dr. BAK NGUYEN & WILLIAM BAK
MASTER CONTROL

THE PANDA
CHAPTER 34- Dr. BAK NGUYEN & WILLIAM BAK
MASTER HARMONY

THE RHINO
CHAPTER 35- Dr. BAK NGUYEN & WILLIAM BAK
MASTER PATIENCE

THE HIPPO
CHAPTER 36 - Dr. BAK NGUYEN & WILLIAM BAK
MASTER DREAMS

THE MONKEY
CHAPTER 37 - Dr. BAK NGUYEN & WILLIAM BAK
MASTER HUMILITY

THE PIG
CHAPTER 38 - Dr. BAK NGUYEN & WILLIAM BAK
MASTER GRATITUDE

THE ELEPHANT
CHAPTER 39 - Dr. BAK NGUYEN & WILLIAM BAK
MASTER AWARENESS

THE FOX
CHAPTER 40 - Dr. BAK NGUYEN & WILLIAM BAK
MASTERING IMAGINATION

THE PARROT
CHAPTER 41 - Dr. BAK NGUYEN & WILLIAM BAK
MASTERING LISTENING

DRAGON HEART
CHAPTER 42 - Dr. BAK NGUYEN & WILLIAM BAK
JUST THE BEGINNING

REVELATION
CHAPTER 43 - Dr. BAK NGUYEN
A NEW ANCHOR

CONCLUSION
BY Dr. BAK NGUYEN

THE JOURNEY OF FATHER AND SON

INTRODUCTION

by Dr. BAK NGUYEN

15 months, 15 books written. That's my personal statement to the world. I won't lie, I never intended to mark such statements nor did I know I had it in me to write and to share as much.

It started on a dare: would I dare to take the stage to speak about my entrepreneurial endeavour... after the former first lady of the United States of America, Michelle Obama?

> "I am a man of my word. I do not back down."
> Dr. Bak Nguyen

So I was stuck with my fears and pride. In truth, I was terrified. I started to prepare TED talks to get prepared for the stage and also to improve my English...

You see, I am a French native speaker. Even today, I think in French first and my head has to translate my thoughts and words.

So I woke up one hour earlier in the morning and started to write. Fear kept me going for a while. Slowly **fear morphed into discipline** and discipline into momentum.

After 2 weeks, I had 21 chapters, an introduction and a conclusion to show. **SYMPHONY OF SKILLS** was born, my first book.

I just set a personal record and maybe also a Guinness to write a book within 2 weeks, only to learn that Michelle Obama wouldn't be making it to the speaking even after all.

Even though it was a miss, I played it perfectly. I bet on myself and I opened a new door, one to my soul. I have to precise that I was writing on top of my usual life both as a CEO and as a dentist.

But now that I had finished my book, with one hour free in my day, **I couldn't just return to sleep**.

The momentum and the discipline pulled me up to a new identity: **writer and thinker**. I went on to write more, about business, about leadership, about identity, about medicine, about power, about momentum, about human evolution, about communication…

One hour a day, or two, that was all it took. One hour, an open mind and 15 books within 15 months is my statement and world record. I will be applying to the Guinness World Records for an official title as soon as my books all reach Amazon.

I won't lie, **FORCES OF NATURE**, my 15th opus was among the hardest ones. You see, until the 11th month, I was having fun writing, not aiming for anything precise. Until I got in my head that I wanted a Guinness title.

At the 11th month of writing, I had 7 books written and only one published. To publish and to sell were not my concern: my talent is to write. So let's write! I wanted to have a good looking number to show, how about 12/12?

12 books within 12 months. But it meant that I would have to write 5 books within the upcoming month. Needless to say that it was simply impossible, at least for someone like me.

With a smile, I still gave myself into the challenge to finish my first year of writing with 9 books to show. The only parts missing were the ones of some of my co-authors and the conclusions which logically have to come by the end of the writing process.

9/12, that's huge, but I did not hit my goal. As my team was working on the editing and the publishing, I kept my pace and kept writing, one chapter at a time.

I know, it's hard to believe that most of the time, at the beginning of my chapter, I had no clue of what would be coming out. As much as I do not plan the topics of my books. One title, one topic at a time, just like my chapters:

> "I am discovering the next step as I talk, as I walk, as I write."
> Dr. Bak Nguyen

From last March, as I started my **YESMAN'S** challenge of 12 months. I started sharing my journey on the social media. Now many people are following my journey, my goals and my deceptions.

To keep the momentum and the communication, I now always start my projects with a title and a cover. As soon as those two are found, the project morphs into a book to be. And it gets published on the social networks.

From last August, I kept my pace writing in average two books a month covering different and diverse topics. By the third week of November, I had a little more than a week and a half to come up with a new subject to start the writing of my final book.

My mentor suggested me to write about my challenges. I didn't think much about the idea but I had no alternative and no time to think.

I went all in. **FORCES OF NATURE**, that would be my final opus before the end of the dateline.

Writing **FORCES OF NATURE** would have two effects. On the Pro side, it should be pretty easy to write since I'd be writing from memories.

On the negative side, it would be such a waste, just like making a movie only comprised of action scenes. It would be expensive and often, would lose much of the value of each scene. I made my cover and I put it out online.

After two days of writing, I felt that something was terribly wrong: I didn't feel anything writing.

If I was sharing my challenges and my fears, I should feel naked, shy, embarrassed, but it wasn't the case. Was I simply too tired to feel? Or was it my writing that wasn't up to the standard? I started to worry.

I asked one of my close counsellors, Brenda Garcia, whose code name is « **my Conscience** » to feed me back. Brenda has read most of my books and is also leading the team for their publishing process.

She went back to me, shy and embarrassed: « Doc, do you think it's worth it to write another book now? » I didn't need to hear more, she confirmed my fears.

The next day, Tranie, my wife woke me up: « Honey, wake up, it's 7 already! » That went through my spine and my soul, 7 already!? »

For the last months, I woke up around 5:30 by myself, without alarm or reminders. Now even my body was telling me that the ride was over.

I panicked, I had already published the title and the cover of **FORCES OF NATURE** on the web. I took a few hours that day with Brenda and went out to save this last endeavour.

FORCES OF NATURE is one of my best works, if not the best of all! I delivered the last words nearly 14 hours before the end of the challenge.

I was exhausted, proud and excited all at once. I could now submit a record for 15 on 15. I did not have to prove myself to anyone anymore, I had done it! But it wasn't about proving myself.

> "As immigrants kids, proving yourself is always somewhere on the table, hardwired into our core beliefs..."
> Dr. Bak Nguyen

It's about doing what felt right. Right! I finished my challenge on Friday, November 30th. I was feeling tall, strong and smart. But there was still a little something...

Now that I am wrapping up 2018, there was still a promise I had made that I hadn't fulfilled yet. About a year earlier, William, my son wanted to write a book. I promised him my help and we came up with a trilogy of **the Chicken, the Lion and the Dragon Heart.**

I tried many times during the last 12 months to find a concept, a structure on which to write the children books. I even started a third of a Hollywood script but I didn't feel my genius there... Now that I stood tall facing the world, how did I stand in front of my kid?

One good night sleep and I went on to tackle that last challenge before the end of the year. For countless times, I went to Indigo-Chapter, the bookstore, to find inspiration... in vain.

That night, inspiration came in with the voice of Siri. I was lost and a little disappointed that I couldn't find a solid base to build on. We knew the concept:

> "We are all born little, as a chicken heart. If we keep an open mind, we will grow into a lion heart. Some will choose to be close-minded and will remain small."
> Dr. Bak Nguyen

I gave William my iPhone, put on Notes and pressed on the mic, the speech-to-text functionality. William started talking, answering the question of **how a chicken can grow into a lion**.

With the text appearing on the screen, he gained in confidence and gave himself completely into the task. He was writing books!

I was fired up and forgot about my fatigue and exhaustion. I went back home and started to make sense of his words, edited them and framed them for the **LEGEND OF THE CHICKEN HEART**.

We would make it by the end of the year! I would finish the year fulfilling that promise I made to William!

Here is the story of the making of the trilogy **LEGEND OF THE CHICKEN HEART, LEGEND OF THE LION HEART** and **LEGEND OF THE DRAGON**.

It is also the story of how I shared my passion and my world with my 8 year-old son and how we evolved together, as father and son and now, co-authors.

This book is about my own experience parenting. The funny thing is that I am still myself a kid who never really grew up...

CHAPTER 1
"THE CHICKEN HEART"
by Dr. BAK NGUYEN

It all started about a year ago while I was writing **LEADERSHIP**, my third book. 21 presidential speeches to save the world. Changing the world with words and hope, that was my mission.

I had no clue if I could do it nor if I had in me to deliver such an endeavour. The book will be available within the next months, I'll let you be the judge. As for me, I am pretty confident.

But before I could say such a bold word, **confident**, I needed to test the speeches. I read them out loud to listen to them and to correct and fine-tune the wording.

Twenty one speeches deep enough to evoke emotions out of the crowd and still vague enough to be adapted to most situations. I was in deep unfamiliar waters.

One concept emerged very strongly from many speeches, the **Lion Heart**. As I was rehearsing out loud, my son, William Bak, who was 7 at that time, caught on the words and the ideas.

From time to time, he saw me writing from my phone, but most of the time, he caught me reading my speeches out loud. I never thought that it would affect him somehow. Until one evening...

We were driving back home from work, exhausted. Tranie was as tired as I was and William was sitting in the back of the car. Suddenly, out of the black, from the backseat, a voice rose.

> "Papa, when I am going to be big,
> I will write 2 books!"
> William Bak

A surge of energy lightened up the entire car! What?! He wanted to write books!? About a lion heart! I never pushed him in any way to follow my footsteps.

I looked in Tranie's eyes and she was falling in love once more! Those were one of these moments you'll never forget how loved you were. Were we surprised, amazed and proud, all at once.

I was so inspired that the next morning I wrote one of my best chapters to date. Usually, I wake up at around 5 AM to shower and to write.

Around 7 AM, I am done and can go on with my usual day. Actually, that is not accurate. By 7, I usually wake up Tranie greeting her with a chapter! Poor Tranie, she had philosophy for breakfast for a while...

That morning, I went into William's room instead and woke him up!

"Buddy, you will not write about a lion heart, that's my book. You will be writing about a chicken heart!" That was a joke, but it had the intended effect.

William became red and argued for a long time about why he should be writing about the **Lion Heart**, the chicken was such an insult to him.

The more he reacted, the more fun I had...

> "Sometimes, I am more of a big brother to my son than a dad..."
> Dr. Bak Nguyen

Just like two kids, we argued for weeks. Day after day, the discussion evolved to the point that I sorted some sense out of it.

I arrived with the concept that we are all born small, with a Chicken heart. If we open our mind to grow, we might grow into a lion heart one day. That hope of growing into a lion rallied William to my cause.

What started as a joke was now a channel allowing me to reach my 7 year-old kid and to teach him concepts and philosophy! I was never a candidate for best dad of the year, but now, I had a way to catch up!

Excited and hopeful, I promised William that we would be writing the Chicken book together. But first, I needed to finish the book that I was currently writing then: **IDENTITY**. He was an enthusiast and showed me support and patience.

By the end of that year, I was through with **IDENTITY**. While I was still writing, I kept on with my conversations with William and slowly we elaborated the chicken concept into 3 stages:

- The **Chicken Heart** who needs an **open mind** to grow.
- The **Lion Heart** who needs an **open heart** to fly. Flying Lions are Dragons.
- The **Dragon Heart** who can change shape if it's **flexible**

The ideas didn't come all at once, but with our ongoing conversation, the ideas were shaping up very clearly to both William and myself.

We would be writing these children's books together. How hard could that be? I couldn't have been more mistaken!

By the beginning of the next year, I went to Punta Cana for a family vacation. I was sure that within a week, I could finish those books, sitting on the beach with William.

I tried, really hard. I came up with, and even wrote, a third of a manuscript for a kid's Hollywood movie trying to illustrate the concept of the Chicken growing into a Lion... but it didn't nail the concept.

William was still talking with me and waiting for signs to join in and collaborate with his dad on his book. Almost a year went by before I could have anything of substance.

That was after I finished my record of 15 on 15. I remembered my unfulfilled promise to William. Him, he was waiting for me to open the subject.

I asked him how would a Chicken grow into a Lion through different subjects. I gave him my phone and he talked through the speech recognition software.

Most of the time, the transcript was useless. But every time he talked, I was listening carefully. I emerged myself into his words and ideas.

I used my **power of Empathy** to write, putting myself in his shoes. I made sense of his 8 year-old logic and words.

The results were astonishing! We were both amazed in front of the beauty of our text and the ease doing it. In an interview, William said that he thought that writing was hard, but with his dad, it was easy.

> "Easy and fun were the keys."
> Dr. Bak Nguyen

I used the **power of momentum** to press on and within a week, 7 chapters of **THE LEGEND OF THE CHICKEN HEART** were completed. William was delivering about two chapters a day, talking to Siri.

Every time, I went on immediately to write, not loosing anything of his essence. Then, I read back the result to him and Tranie to keep their interest and amazement.

From William's eyes, I sensed the satisfaction and confidence building up. You see, William is more of an Anglophone growing up with YouTube and Netflix.

We, his mom and I, are mainly French speakers, but we both are functional in English.

Until lately, we found it pretty amusing that our son who was born in Canada had to adapt to the French policy of education… like an immigrant.

We stopped laughing the day that he had difficulties in class passing his french lessons. That struggle haunted the three of us for more than three years.

I do not want to put any extra burden on my kid, he is 8 and speaks currently three languages! How many of his teachers can say the same? But it was not about pride here, but about confidence.

> "I am pretty aware of the importance of Confidence in a kid's development, of self-confidence."
> Dr. Bak Nguyen

That day, we were at the 6th chapter of **THE LEGEND OF THE CHICKEN HEART**. As I drove him to school, he said proudly to his mom: "Mama, I may have difficulties in French but I can write books!"

He left for school confident and happy as we never saw him before. That was a blessing from the sky!

Sure, I was trying to keep my promise to my kid, but to predict that it would heal his confidence was an unexpected surprise and surely a very welcomed one.

That night I had an interview scheduled at home with a friend and podcaster. We were supposed to cover my last win of 15 on 15. I shared with him William's story and how he was writing books with me.

It got the intended effect, the interview was turned on William and the web went crazy about the kid! He stole my thunder!!!

William spoke in French for the whole interview, sharing his views and experience writing. I was so proud of my little kid, the chicken heart! He behaved as a real lion, a baby lion, perhaps?

I used the interview to write the last chapters of **Chicken Heart** and voilà! William had just completed his first book within less than a week with the help of his father. He is 8.

Wait a minute, isn't that another Guinness record? I started to realize how big was actually my promise to William and the ripple effect of Chicken Heart.

That gave me the idea of getting him on the podium with me, as we would be celebrating my first Guinness record by scoring another one, and the second one, William would be joining me: to write 6 children's books within a month, 3 in French and 3 in English!

I will never
FORCE YOU. I WILL SHOW YOU.
...
William Bak

ACT I
THE LEGEND OF THE
CHICKEN HEART

"A CHICKEN HEART NEEDS TO BE OPEN MINDED TO GROW"
by Dr. Bak Nguyen & William Bak

CHAPTER 2
"EAT TO GROW"

by Dr. Bak Nguyen & William Bak

So this is the book
Of the chicken heart.
This is the beginning
Of something new,
Something great!

Do you want to learn
How to grow your
Chicken heart?

I am little.
I am a chicken heart.
Yes, we are all born little.

To grow, we must
Be open minded
And we will grow one day
Into a lion heart.

Some will not be open
And will stay small.
That's what my dad told me.
And I believe him.

> "To grow you must eat.
> Open your mind just like
> you open your mouth."
> - William Bak

First, you have to study hard.
Not just work hard,
But work smart too.

And to be smart,
We need to be open minded.

It starts with food.
If I eat a lot,
I'll grow as much

But if I am not open minded
I'll always eat the same food
Until I do not want to eat it
Anymore

And then,
I'll grow less,
I'm not strong
anymore.

> "If I am open minded, there is always something new to eat!"
> – William Bak

I can eat many things
And I will always grow stronger
My dad said
It's the same thing with school.

If I am open minded,
I will grow smarter.

One day, I will grow
Into a lion heart.
Smart and strong.

CHAPTER 3
"WHEN IT'S HARD IT'S TIME FOR ME TO LEARN"

by Dr. Bak Nguyen & William Bak

Family is important
Because my family
Helps me to grow.

When my dad and my mom
Are hard on me
I do not like it.

But I understand that they are
Teaching me something new.
They do not want to hurt me.

"When my parents are hard with me, they want me to learn so I can grow."
— William Bak

Sometimes, they are even harder on me
Because I did not listen
I know, it's my fault.

If I want them to stop being hard
I have to say that I am sorry.
With that, the hard is gone
And happiness is back!

I always want my family
To be happy!
Because I love my family.

Every time I see the hard coming
I know that it is time for me to learn.

I'll tell you a secret.
Sometimes I do it
Because I love my parents,
So my family can be happy.

I can grow eventually
From a Chicken Heart
Into a Lion Heart.

"Family is important!"
- William Bak

CHAPTER 4
"DANCE TO BE HAPPY"
by Dr. Bak Nguyen & William Bak

When I need to grow,
I dance.
Dancing is action.

Every time I dance,
Things are becoming real.

When I dance,
Things are coming out.
Good things and sometimes,
Bad things.
But they are out!

"I feel better and then,
I dance even more I dance!"
- William Bak

Sometimes at school,
I cannot dance.
I have to hold it
Until I can go out.

Once outside,
I am dancing
And I am happy!

I hate conflicts.
Each time I dance,
There is no more conflict.
At least inside.

"And I am ready to go back in
and to learn more, with an open mind."
- William Bak

I know that to grow into a lion heart
I must learn new things
And grow from them.

If I am happy, it's easier.
And if I am not happy,

> "I dance until I am happy!"
> - William Bak

This is how
I will not stay
A chicken heart.

If I dance all the time,
I will become
A Lion heart!

CHAPTER 5
"TRUTH GOOD, LIE BAD"

by Dr. Bak Nguyen & William Bak

This is about
Talking the truth,
Always.

When I talk,
I like to tell the truth.
It feels better.

When I lie,
I do not do that often,
Only sometimes.

I do not feel great
Because I do not like
How people look at me.

It makes me feel little.
If I feel little for too long,
I might stay small forever!

"To grow, I must have an open mind."
- William Bak

I am just a chicken heart!
I must grow to become
One day, a lion heart!

So no lying to feel better.
Just tell the truth, it's easier
And it feels good.

Try it! Everyday!
That's what my dad told me.

And everyday, I try my best
To grow into a lion heart.
By telling the truth,
Always.

"If I feel little for too long,
I might stay small forever!
That's why I don't lie"

— William Bak

CHAPTER 6
"BE COOL TO BE SMOOTH"

by Dr. Bak Nguyen & William Bak

Be cool,
That's what my dad said.
Actually, he said cool down.
It's pretty much the same.

By being cool,
A chicken can grow
Into a lion heart!

Because cool is smooth.
If you are smooth,
You can walk faster
That's true.

If you are smooth,
You can just slide
Instead of walking.

I love to slide,
It's faster and easier.
My dad always said
That fast is good.
To slide is fast,
You need to be cool
First.

Don't try to impress your friends.
That is not cool!
Because sometimes,
It's not true!

> "You know what's not cool?
> Being ungrateful!"
> - William Bak

When somebody gives you something,
Be grateful and say thank you.
Everyone will be happy.

Forget to say thank you
And someone will be sad.
Sometimes, even mad.

I prefer to share with my friends.
Everyone is happier when I shared.
My dad is proud of me,
And I am happy!

"Be cool to be happy.
And when I am happy,
I am open to grow."
- William Bak

CHAPTER 7
"NO LOSER, JUST LEARNER"

by Dr. Bak Nguyen & William Bak

I am a kid.
I like to play,
And playing is good!

When you can play with your friends,
You have to respect the rules.

> "And if you lose, don't complain!"
> - William Bak

I like to win.
But when I lose,
I must learn
So I'll win next time.
It's just a game

To have fun,
Everybody needs to win.
If not today, then tomorrow.

If a friend is losing
Don't say that he is a loser.
That's not nice.
Maybe tomorrow, I'll be losing
I don't want my friends
To call me a loser.

Yesterday, I didn't win.
I didn't feel bad
Because my friends didn't say
That I was a loser.

Just not the winner
... that time.
But we still had fun.
It was just a game.

I told a joke to be funny.
Everyone laughed,
Everyone loved me,
Even if I didn't win.
I end up making more friends.

That's how I grew a little bigger,
Slowly into a lion heart.

"Remember, you did not lose
if you learned something new."
- William Bak

CHAPTER 8
"THE COURAGE TO FOLLOW YOUR DREAMS"

by Dr. Bak Nguyen & William Bak

In my dreams,
I am already
A dragon heart.

When I wake up,
I am still just
A chicken heart.

This is the last chapter,
I'll be a lion heart
After this book.

I am excited, about dreaming.
I opened my mind to grow.
That I know.

To know where to go
I sometimes follow my dreams.
Not the nightmares,
Only the good dreams.

To make a dream come true,
Don't just use your head.
Most of the time,
It is not enough.
Use your heart,
it is more powerful!

I saw my dad build his dreams.
He used his heart first,
And his head after.

If you have the courage
To follow your dreams,
They will come true!

"To have courage,
you need a good heart."
- William Bak

My dad always told me to believe.
I believe my dad,
I believe in my dreams,
I believe in me.

> "Go forward and
> don't look back, ever."
> - William Bak

That's why I will soon be,
A lion heart.
Because I move forward
With an open mind
And a big heart!

Big enough to believe,
Big enough to have many friends,
Big enough to meet new people.

I am a chicken heart,
I have grown stronger, smarter
And bigger!

CHAPTER 9
"LEARN, EAT AND GROW"

by Dr. Bak Nguyen & William Bak

A chicken maybe little,
But little is good,
Because the chicken learns fast.
Faster and faster!

Until you become a lion heart,
All you have to do is to be open mind.
Learn, Eat and Grow!

My secret to keep growing
Is to always finish all that I started.
It takes actions, real actions.

I know I will finish.
So I can start new things
To keep growing.

> "You need to continue everything you started."
> – William Bak

If I do not finish one thing,
It becomes messy.
Then I have to clean up.

I don't like to clean up.
So I finish everything
I started.

It's just like the food on your plate.
Finish it, that's what our moms
Always say.

> "Do it! Wait for nothing!
> Go make your dreams
> come true"
> – William Bak

I wrote this book, so everyone
Can be smarter, can learn how
To become a lion heart.

What I learned writing this book
Is the **Head** is some times stupid.
It is not as important as the **Heart**.

The **Heart** is the most important.
To grow your heart
Is the most important thing.

We all share the same blood.
That's why everyone can learn to
Become a lion heart.

It's your choice,
You just need to be
Open-minded!

> "The more fun I have,
> the more I will be open,
> the more I will grow!"
> - William Bak

CHAPTER 10
"THE SUPER CHICKEN"
by Dr. BAK NGUYEN

What I learned writing **Chicken Heart** with William is that our kids will always surprise us. They know much more than what they are showing or what we expect from them.

Mainly, they copy what and who they see. I know, no big revelations until now, but those are facts too often overlooked.

> "Whatever you want to teach your kids, do it first. Master it and they will follow your example."
> Dr. Bak Nguyen

This is mainly how I succeeded to interest my kid in writing, not having a clue that my actions would inspire him. Today, what he is looking to do is to be me.

His exact words, Papa, I want to be you! I am both flattered and proud but I know better, soon enough he will want to beat me!

And that's okay, that will only mean that the kid will have become the master... only to discover that to get to the next stage, the master will have to accept to become a student once again, sometimes, studying under his former protege...

You have no idea how much I've grown from this experience writing with my kid. Listening and seeing the world through his eyes was enlightening.

"If you want to live forever,
try empathy of the youth."
Dr. Bak Nguyen

I had the impression that both my mind and my heart were having an youth therapy. **Empathy**, to see the world through someone else's eyes and to understand their feelings.

Soon enough you will discover what you knew from a completely new angle.

Kids are pretty quick to emulate what they see. While writing **THE LEGEND OF THE CHICKEN HEART**, William surprised me by taking control without me noticing it.

While I was the one teaching him how to be a good person on the path of the Lion Heart, he decided that he would return the favour.

My wife and I had some couple issues and we were fighting often, sometimes in front of the kid. Nothing serious, just some frustrations and, with the accumulated fatigue, sometimes we said things we didn't mean.

William reacted to it. As he wrapped up one of the first chapters of **Chicken Heart**, he went on to give me advice, about how I should be happy, how to keep my heart light so I could fly one day!

That's it! That was it! William just gave birth to the **Lion Heart** book, about how a chicken will be helping the Lion, his dad, to fly one day!

It was a genius stroke, but I have to admit, William had most of the merits. So we went on to write **THE LEGEND OF THE LION HEART** simultaneously with **THE LEGEND OF THE CHICKEN HEART**.

His love and his words got me at my core. With my power of **Empathy**, I went all in into my feelings from the kid's point of view.

That helped me tremendously to reassess my behaviours and their logic. In a few words, **I became a better man thanks to him.**

It also brought the writing of the second book to a whole new level: one where the Lion has to learn from the Chicken.

> "To have an open mind is step one.
> To keep growing, one needs an open heart."
> Dr. Bak Nguyen

We need to keep that heart open to grow it and to keep it light. At the end of **THE LEGEND OF THE CHICKEN HEART**, I introduced a new concept, the **super chicken**!

That was a new concept, a trap in which the chicken will grow in strength and intelligence but with a chicken heart, a small heart.

Is the super chicken an alternative to the lion, absolutely not since it still remains a chicken, only bigger and stronger. But unfortunately, in real life, it is often a possibility.

> "What makes a Lion is his heart."
> Dr. Bak Nguyen

In our society, many people **confuse strength and nobility, smartness with courage, trade with generosity**. Only people with a heart, a real heart might understand the nuances and the differences.

A super chicken is no leader nor hero. A super chicken is simply a bigger chicken. Déjà vu? Are we following and idolizing super chickens or Lion Hearts?

This is a hard question to face and facing it might explain a lot.

> "The super chicken is a dead end from the evolutionary standpoint."
> Dr. Bak Nguyen

William asked me that question. Can a super chicken fly?

THE HOUSE OF
LIONS

CHAPTER 11
"THE LION HEART"
by Dr. BAK NGUYEN

Today is Xmas. It's William's 8th Xmas and surely, one of the most amazing ones. Throughout the last years, I gave my son the best and all of what I would have loved to have.

He swims in abundance, love and toys.

> "Where do we draw the line between abundance and spoil?"
> Dr. Bak Nguyen

On that, my views are radically different. I chose to teach him wealth, swimming in abundance, he would have to learn to manage and to organize, not looking at one but at many. That's what I told myself for years... Actually, I was simply projecting.

8 years ago, around this time of the year, William was about 6 months when I had to cover the night shift feeding him. I fed him around midnight and again at around 5 AM.

I was living in a condo-hotel on the last floor with a view of the sunrise over the bridge and river. I had that wonder for years but I only enjoyed its beauty as I became a father.

You see, I am a heavy sleeper. I love to sleep. So to wake up every morning before sunrise was a challenge, a real challenge for me. But what do you know?

> "As a dad, you find Will you didn't know you had in you..."
> Dr. Bak Nguyen

To wake up at 5 to feed William who would soon fall asleep after he finished his bottle left me much time to enjoy the view and to think. I had to leave for work at around 7, by the time he finished drinking, it was around 5:45, not enough time to return to bed... and above all, he slept so comfortably in my arms.

Those mornings were real blessings to allow me to enjoy the present and what I had received from God.

Looking at William sleep so peacefully with a ray of sunlight tickling his face, I wanted nothing but the best for him. I also remembered the difficult relationship I have with my dad, despite the love we have for each other.

Would I repeat the same path with William? To wake up happily at 5 AM took more than Will, it took love, pure love. I suddenly felt gratitude pumping up in my heart and flooding through my veins.

I understood the depth of my father's love and now felt how it feels to be a dad. I loved him even more, but he wasn't there to hear me say it. Only William was there.

Even if he had been there, he wouldn't have been listening, always too busy to show me where I went wrong... That is how he is built. That is why we are not so close...

But this little guy sleeping in my arms, would he end up just like my dad and I, loving each other through mind games and self-imposed challenges?

And I am so much tougher than my dad, I do have a will of steel and a passion of fire bending everything, including my own Will! Will-I-am, what will you be? How will we evolve together?

The signs were too obvious to ignore, the danger was imminent. If I kept the current trend, I would give William all of the best only to ask for the impossible in return, all wrapped with love and good intentions...

I knew better, I've suffered most of my life in that lie and faulty belief. That morning, I took a cornerstone of my past and threw it away.

> "I will not expect anything. I will do and hope. Worst case scenario, I will have been."
> Dr. Bak Nguyen

In simple words, whatever I wish for him, I will do it first, I will be first. Smart and strong, I will keep training every minute of each day.

Generous and kind, I will be judging myself in the mirror every morning as I get out of the shower and every night before going to bed. Flexible is the new norm...

> "I was steel. I knew fire. It was time for me
> to combine the two of them. Will and love."
> Dr. Bak Nguyen

William gave me my wings, larger and more powerful than ever before since I was now finding my place as a dad, not just proving my worth to my parents or to the world, but to my son and to myself.

That decision changed the course of my life from above average to leader and alpha.

"Leadership and an Alphaness are gifts received at birth. Nevertheless, to shine they need to be accepted and polished continuously."
Dr. Bak Nguyen

That was my first day as a chicken heart, a chicken dad. I opened up myself to learn and to be, to become better and better. It was never enough, there was always something new to learn and to master.

The world is such a great and vast place. I started to see the world through William's perspective, for the first time, once again, but with the wisdom and the means at my disposal to make things happen.

Something truly magical happened, I was growing at a scary pace. When we say that kids are growing quickly, that's an understatement to my pace of learning and mastering. I grew up side by side with William.

I didn't have to teach him much, he just looked and me and felt the truth and the vibe of pure energy. That forged our bond as father and son.

Several years later, he simply picked up on who I became to discover the world and the endless possibilities. The chicken heart was born, this time, into a book. Was I a lion heart? I guessed, I wished.

> "Greater than the sum of its parts…"
> ARISTOTLE

Make it happen and be open to embrace the results… and to course correct by adapting quickly. William, as he was dictating his views about how to grow from a Chicken to a Lion based on my questions and my teachings, started something else.

He loves to teach back. While I was teaching him in the Legend of the Chicken Heart, he started new chapters telling what to do to be happy. That wasn't the first time, by 5, he had already added **"to be happy"** to my list of things to be.

> "Be strong, be smart, be kind, be generous and be flexible. To that, he added, be happy."
> Dr. Bak Nguyen and William Bak

Now at 8, he was showing me how to keep my heart open and lighten it up, flushing the burden and the weights. His words were so simple and yet made so much sense that I had a hard time resisting them. When he added: The Kid has become the master!

I felt the revelation to my own story, my own legend. To bend my Will of steel without suffering, I didn't need the fire of passion, but the warmth of love was more than enough.

> "The warmth of love opened my heart
> to accept the teaching of a kid."
> Dr. Bak Nguyen and William Bak

At 8 years old. I made sense of his thoughts, but the core was him, truly him taking my hand and bridging his soul into the bond, our bond as father and son, now as buddies and co-authors.

Love took all the available place, there was just no space left for even the shadow of Pride.

The power and the light were such that we finished both books, the **Chicken Heart** and the **Lion Heart** simultaneously within a week.

It was the best time of my life, sharing magical thoughts with my son. Just like when he was sleeping in my arms at sunrise, today, he became that ray of sunshine.

Writing those lines, I can see his babyface of 6 months smiling as the sun caressed his cheek and mine.

We are not better nor smarter than anyone. We simply let go and gave into each other.

> "I love, I believe and I bet on myself."
> Dr. Bak Nguyen

William picked up on the clues and followed the example. He loves, believes and learns to bet... right now on his dad. With William's faith in me, I feel that nothing is out of reach, nothing is impossible.

Sure, I had that in me before, but now, it can be done with ease, smoothly and without pain. The fire of evolution has just been replaced with the warmth and the light of pure love and the hope of a child.

To William, I love you with all my heart. Thank you, my son.

William , I salute you!

ACT II
THE LEGEND OF THE
LION HEART

"A LION HEART NEEDS TO KEEP HIS HEART OPEN TO FLY ONE DAY"
by Dr Bak Nguyen & William Bak

CHAPTER 12
"LEARN TO LAUGH"
by Dr. Bak Nguyen & William Bak

I'm a kid,
And I'm still
A chicken heart.

My dad is a Lion heart.
He is strong and smart,
But still, he cannot fly.
Only a dragon heart can fly.

So today, I will help
My dad to become
a Dragon Heart.

You see, my dad
Is always working.
Even after work,
He comes back home
He works more.

He is always serious.
That's too heavy.
So I told him to have fun
With me.

But most of the time,
He is too busy working more.

One day, I got angry,
Because he promised me
That we would have fun
Together.

> "Papa, if you want to fly one day,
> you need to have fun!"
> — William Bak

I will teach my dad how to fly!
If he is always serious,
He is too heavy.

If he has fun and laughs,
The words are getting out
Instead of staying inside his heart.

The more they are coming out,
The lighter he gets!
And he will fly when he is
Light enough!

"The more he laughs, the lighter he gets! That's how he will fly away one day!"
- William Bak

The kid has become
The master!

CHAPTER 13
"BEING GRATEFUL"
by Dr. Bak Nguyen & William Bak

Be Grateful
Sometimes my dad
Is not happy.

He is talking harsh
To me and my mom.
Each time, I try to give him
My love.

Sometimes it works,
Sometimes, it's not enough.

I told him to be grateful to us.
I want him to stop being mad.
If he is happy and less serious,
He will laugh more,
And everyone will be happy!

"If you laugh, everyone can be happy!"
- William Bak

By being grateful,
He can enjoy us.
And we can smile
With him.
Together, we will be
A happy family.

The problem is that
He works too hard.
So I told him
To have fun,
And to let go.

Tomorrow, he can work more.
With some fun in the day,
He will be happy and grateful.
And he will feel better.

If he feels better,
The lion heart will grow.
The day he can fly,
He will become
A dragon heart

"By being grateful, he will feel better and one day, fly because he has become a dragon heart."
- William Bak

The kid has become
The master!

CHAPTER 14
"FIRST YOU NEED TO RELAX"
by Dr. Bak Nguyen & William Bak

First, you need to relax
Sit down and breathe.
To be happy, you need to have
Some good times.

You can even sleep, if you want.
Everybody needs to sleep at night.

> "Even in the day, you can sleep
> when you are tired."
> - William Bak

My dad works a lot.
He is tired all the time.
That's because even when
He comes back from work,

He works more.

That's why
He is so serious.
Because he is tired.

If he relaxes a little bit
The pressure will get out
From his mouth
And from his heart.

> "Even if his heart is big,
> it cannot hold too much stuff."
> — William Bak

So sleep papa.
You will feel better
Better enough
To be happy.

> "And happy enough to grow
> into a dragon heart."
> — William Bak

The student has become
The master!

CHAPTER 15
"TO TRY SOMETHING NEW"

by Dr. Bak Nguyen & William Bak

This is about listening.
My dad always wants
Me to listen to him.

I do my best everyday.
I've grown pretty good
Doing so!

But sometimes,
I think he should listen to me.
You see, I know what he wants.

> "He wants to grow
> into a dragon and fly."
> *- William Bak*

But he never flew until now.
He keeps doing the same thing
Day after day.

That's why he cannot fly.
Not yesterday, not today,
Not tomorrow!

But I know,
If he listens to his kid,
I know how to fly!
I'll show him.

> "All he needs is to listen,
> to try something new, my way!"
> - William Bak

He always said
That to grow,
I must be open.
So be open dad!
Listen to me.

To try is good
Try again
And try better.

That's how he will learn
Something new.
That's what he taught me!

One day, he will fly,
I know it!
As a lion heart who becomes
A dragon heart.

> "That day, I will be so proud of him.
> My dad, the dragon heart."
> - William Bak

The kid has become
The master!

CHAPTER 16
"BE CALM"

by Dr. Bak Nguyen & William Bak

Papa, you are my hero
When you make things happen.
You are more impressive
When you are Calm.

When you are happy,
You can make everything possible!
When you are calm,
You build my dreams
And yours.

"Because you are the boss.
Because you are in control!"

- William Bak

When you are angry,
You are scary.
Even more to a Chicken
Looking at a Lion.

The Lion is supposed
To protect the chicken.
Not scare him.

When you roar,
The others are afraid.
But that's not cool
Papa!

You are a builder.
You built great things.
You are good, building
But you cannot build
When you are angry.

You are kind, papa.
You are a great dad.
You are my best friend.
But you are none of that
When you are angry!

> "It's like you are not the same,
> like you've lost your lion heart."
> – William Bak

When you are angry
It's like Halloween.
You are scary
Even without a costume.

After your Anger,
You always run fast,
To grow back into
A lion heart.
Then, you are calm again.

You are wasting time papa!
It is easier to just grow
Into a dragon heart
Instead of running back.

Could you just
Not be angry?
I'll promise to be
A good kid!

> "If you stay angry, one day,
> you may lose your lion heart
> for good."
> – William Bak

I like you
When you are strong,
When you are smart,
When you make me laugh,
So we can both grow together.

> "Be calm Papa, not angry.
> Be happy, not too serious."
> – William Bak When you are smart

Papa, I love you
I want you to become
A dragon heart
Just take my love
And let's fly together

Oh, wait...
Neither of us can fly yet!

How about you run
While I stand on your shoulders?
See, I made you laugh!
The Chicken and the Lion,
What a great family!

The kid has become
The master!

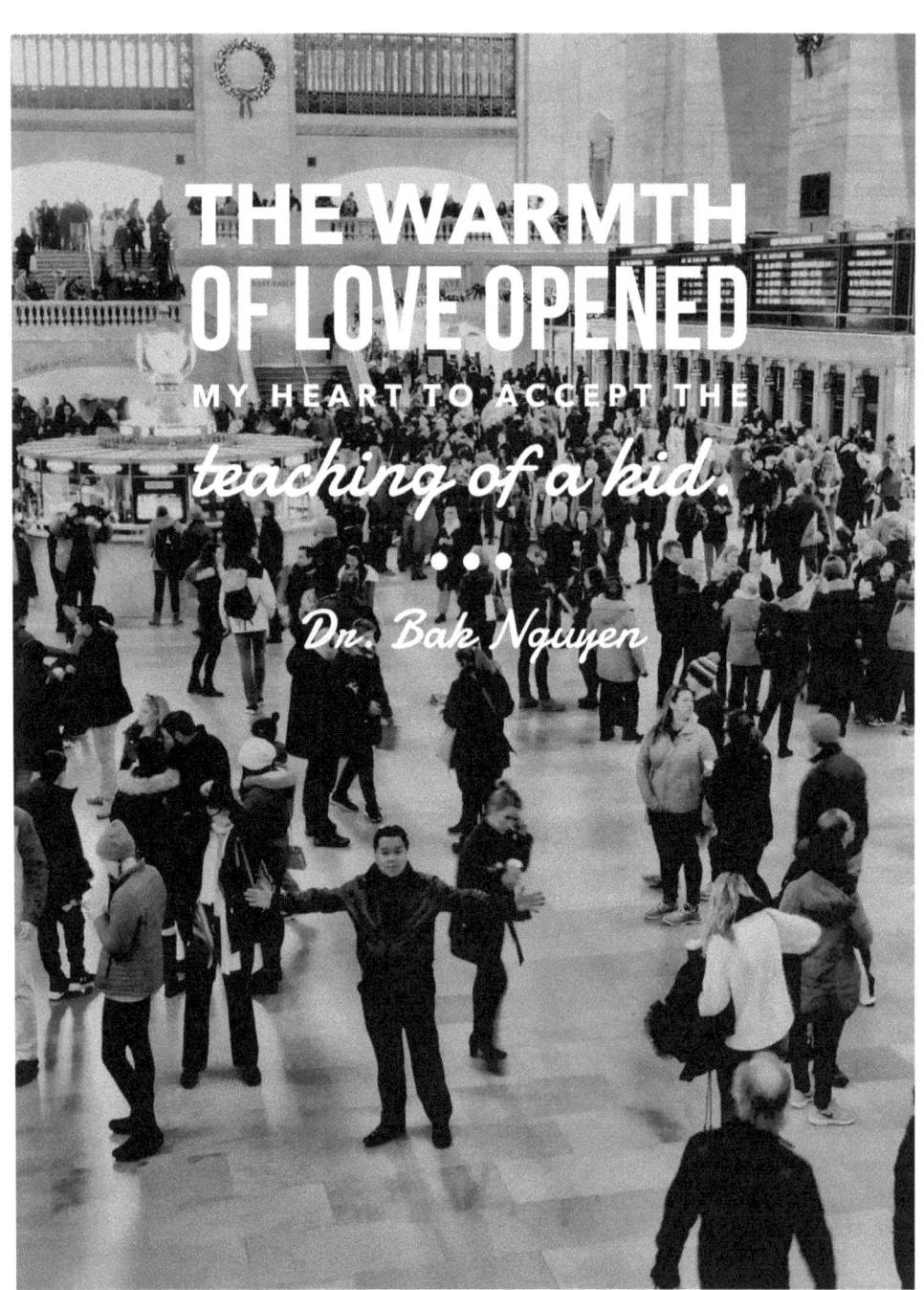

CHAPTER 17
"A BIG HEART"

by Dr. Bak Nguyen & William Bak

I know papa,
Today you are sad.
Even if you are not crying,
I can see it in your eyes.

You have a big heart
And someone hurt it.
Can your heart be too big?

Maybe that's why
People can hurt you.
Even a lion can be hurt?!

I don't like to see you sad.
What can I do
To make you happy?

But papa, I like it
When your heart is big!
Please keep it big
So it can keep growing.

> "Sing Papa, let out the words,
> you'll feel better."
> – William Bak

I like to dance
To let things out.
You can dance too!

But you like to sing.
Sing and I will sing
with you.

Dance and I will
Dance with you.
Be happy
So I can be happy too.

When you are sad,
You make me sad too.
I don't like to be sad.

But I know,
Sometimes it happens.
It's part of life.

> *"But you told me that our life is for us to decide!"*
> *– William Bak*

I decide to be happy.
I decided for you too!
Be happy!

Sing to let your heart feel better.
Dance to make your body
Feel like flying.

You were sad,
Now, be happy.
With the same heart,
With your lion heart,
Papa!

As a chicken heart,
I need to keep my mind open.
As a lion heart,
You need to keep your heart open.

> "Take my love so we can
> fly away together."
> – William Bak

The day we both
Become dragon hearts,
As father and son,
As best buddies.
We will race in the sky
And I will beat you :)

The kid has become
The master!

CHAPTER 18
"ENJOY TODAY"

by Dr. Bak Nguyen & William Bak

Enjoy your day papa!
You are a wizard.
You make things
Come true.

You give your love
But when it's time
For the applauses,
You are not here.

You are always working.
Mama said that you live in tomorrow.
Why papa?I need you today!

When you are here,
Everything is great!
When you are happy,
We have fun!
And when we do,

The day is too short.

> "Enjoy the day to be happy."
> – William Bak

Mama said to be happy.
We must live today,
To enjoy the day, papa.
You deserve it!

I want to share
So many things with you.
If only you were there.

It's okay, if you have to work.
After work, I'll be waiting.
Is that a deal?

When you speak
And tell your stories,
You draw pictures
In my head.

I love the pictures.
Sometimes, I see them
In my dreams.

You showed me
That one day,
I will fly!

Every night, in my dreams,
I am flying, with you!
We are both dragon hearts!

Can we do this for real, papa?
Show me how to fly
To become a dragon heart.
Today, now, I am here.

"To enjoy is to fly!"
- William Bak

Trust me, papa,
I know.
You must believe.
You must be happy.
You must be here today,
And you'll fly!

I saw it last night,
And the night before.

I know papa,
Trust me!

Mama told us to start the day
With 3 good things to tell
Each other.

Here are mine:
I flew with you yesterday.
I want to fly with you today.
We will race in the sky
Tomorrow!

Enjoy papa.
It will make you happy.
Stop trying to fly,
You are already a dragon heart.
You just need to stop
To see it.

"Keep your heart light and open
and you will fly."
- William Bak

You make my dreams come true.
You show me how to build my dreams.
Now I wish that you can
Enjoy my dreams with me.

You don't need to know all the way.
We can come back and try again.
It's fun flying!

I am still a chicken heart.
They say chicken can't fly.

With you, it's easy.
Just like writing,
It's easy when you are around.

So let's fly, together.
Let's fly forever .
You'll show me where
I'll show you how.

The kid has become
The master!

CHAPTER 19
"JUST THE BEGINNING"

by Dr. Bak Nguyen & William Bak

I am growing with you.
Even a kid, a chicken heart
Can learn to fly.

Thanks to you,
My lion heart daddy,
This time, I learn to fly.

Not because you teach me
But because I teach you!

I am grateful
To have you to teach.
Just like you have me
To teach to.

The kid has become the master.
Because the master accepted
To be a good student.
Are you a good student ,papa?

From a lion to a dragon.
It's beautiful to see.
I am so proud of you papa!

I know, I am still a chicken heart.
I've improved much lately.
I am learning fast,
Especially when I am
Teaching you.

When you fly,
I am flying with you.
You show me the sensation,
The wind in my face, the freedom
And the happiness.

> "That's why I want to fly
> with you every day."
> – William Bak

I am a chicken
And I can fly!
Because my daddy is a dragon.
One day, I will become

A dragon too!
For now, I am growing
Into a lion first.

So what's next papa?
Please finish my training
As a lion heart,
So I can finally grow
From Chicken to Lion.

I helped you to become a dragon.
Remember that.
Now it's your turn,
Make my dreams come true.
Help me to become a lion
So I can one day, start
Learning to fly.

I know how, papa
I was your teacher.
Now you have to
Come back as mine.

> "It's fun when we change roles, and then, change it again. It's fun because it's a game."
> – William Bak

I cannot wait to wake up.
To see what will be next.
Every day is dragon's training
With you.

Every day is lion's training
with me.
Every day we are together,
To have fun, to enjoy,
To be happy!

Now that you are a dragon papa,
Where do we go?

CHAPTER 20
"GIVE AND YOU SHALL RECEIVE"
by Dr. BAK NGUYEN

I intentionally spaced out the writing of these chapters to gain more depth and understanding of my feelings about my journey with William, my journey as a dad.

You see, everything is a first to the both of us. That's how we connected together, as two children discovering the world, for the first time.

Usually, I wrote the chapters of a book, one after the next, not jumping a day. The Book of Legends is a different project to me, a more personal one.

Yes, I am still sharing my thoughts and feelings unfiltered, but I also wanted to let the emotions and the sensations sink in before making sense of them.

> "I have become a better father and a better person since I now let my feelings sink in first."
> Dr. Bak Nguyen

Gratitude is my first feeling. The gratitude to have such a wonderful child to exchange and to build with. The gratitude to have taken this journey as a young dad and not a young grandpa.

Time is surely a pricey commodity and I am glad that I took the time to sort out my own priorities. On the matter, I have to thank Tranie, my wife and best friend.

To sort our priorities, this might be the single wiser thing I said until now. My mentor keeps reminding me that time is abundant and also very difficult to keep a grasp on for a long time.

> "Time is like water, it is all around and so easily wasted."
> Dr. Bak Nguyen

The time I spent with William, connecting with him and getting into his world was so rewarding on so many levels that I don't even know where to start.

I told you before that William has his own challenges about learning and mastering three different languages at school. The newest language and the hardest for him to grasp is French.

In the beginning, Tranie and I found it funny and we even joked about our kid being an immigrant... we know that our son is a smart one.

But after three years struggling at school, after having to move him out of a private school to have access to more services in the public system and keep struggling on a daily basis, that was an unexpected challenge for all three of us.

I failed my first French test in high school once. I had to beg for an extra assignment to just barely have the mention passed on my school report. Until I graduated from dental school, my English was still so-so and never would I have thought to become an author.

Today I am among the few authors who can write books at a frenzy pace in both languages, French and English. I do not even make the difference anymore. I hold a few World records on the matter and until lately, I sucked in literature and grammar.

I surely respect the work of the teachers but I do not think that it is a matter of life and death to succeed at school. That's on paper. Somewhere deep inside,

I still have my immigrant genes who will not allow my kid to fail.

> "Confidence is my priority. His confidence."
> Dr. Bak Nguyen

To make sense of his difficulties, his evolution and his success, it all boils down to confidence. For the last 8 years, I made it my priority every time it came down to William.

Of course, I am the disciplinary face of my couple. I am also the every day's Santa and now his BFF. His words, not mine. Best friends forever. But how did I manage to arrive at that level?

It started way before we talked about writing books together. I have an in-ground pool in the back of my house. William was only one when we moved in.

The pool was a big security concern, but it also gave the house its charm. Right from the beginning, I got in my mind that either William would know how to swim or he would be afraid of the water. In both cases, he would be safe.

So I took upon my shoulders to initiate my son to swimming. At the beginning, it was a fight. I was fighting to understand where he would be standing, in or out of the water. He was fighting for his life.

With much efforts and the help of his mom, Tranie, we finally got him comfortable in the water, three years later.

Then, as he was swimming, I gave him a target: to catch me! I usually play the shark in the water, grabbing him by the legs and tickling him. As we reversed roles, he was delighted to be in power. Then came the Transformers...

Two years ago, I had a personal challenge: to swim at least 20 laps every day of the summer. Sunny and rainy, day or night, it didn't matter. I was out dropping my 20 laps.

From day to day, some extras too if I found it in me. My pool is about 40 feet long. It's not the Olympic's standard, the challenge came more on finding the motivation to keep doing the laps day after day... often after long surgery hours.

By Friday night or in the weekend, William joined me and swam with me. He was hooked on transformers back then. He still is today if I stop and think about it.

Nonetheless, that was his biggest motivation. So I played the card: for every 10 laps he would swim with me, I would get him a transformer. We finished that day with 70 laps each, both father and son.

That was my first revelation about how my kid could push me to better myself. Of course, he got his transformers and not the cheap kind, the masterpiece ones! Those I wanted for myself, even as a grown up.

From that point on, we established our special bond from father and son to partners. What I wanted him to be, I became first. As a father, leading by example was not only giving results, it also paid back in more than one way!

I used the same strategy to motivate him at school. Actually, the strategy came as an unexpected and great surprise. As the temperature dropped by the end of that summer, I transferred my momentum from the pool to my dedication in writing. Laps became chapters, consistently, every day or almost.

Then after three months and three books, William picked on the clues and wanted to write too. Put things in perspective, William was 7 years old having difficulties at school and undervalued for his knowledge of three different languages... he is handicapped with his late exposure to French which is the primary, almost the only standard at school.

As I finished my own world record, 15/15, Tranie reminded me of my priorities sorting. By the same time, my mentors all reminded me how lonely it is to be among the top 1%.

A mentor even advised me to slow down if I did not want to lose most of the people around me... but I am a tornado. I do not slow down, ever.

> "If anything, I speed up to keep feeding my momentum."
> Dr. Bak Nguyen

I had a choice to make, but I trained myself never to choose. I want it all! So I tried the pool's strategy on William again, only with a different wrapping.

One week after the completion of my world record 15/15, I had an interview scheduled in the Mdex Mansion. The podcaster is a good friend of mine, Jonas Diop and was pretty open about what I had to share.

As he was expecting me to talk about my recent achievements, I introduced William and the 4 children books we were writing together back then. Jonas quickly found interest in William and the interview shifted focus.

In a word, William stole my thunder! He received three times my views on social media. He did the whole interview in French since Jonas' podcast is French base. Listening to William talk in the podcast, I had to laugh to hide my tears of joy as a father.

He had already finished 2 books by then. The Legend of the Chicken heart and the Legend of the Lion heart, in both languages, French and English.

That gave him 4 books under his belt as a co-author, at 8 and within just a week. He knew that we would be writing the Legend of the Dragon heart right after.

So we set up a new goal for the both of us, live on camera. To establish a new world record, writing 6 children's books within a month.

Actually, we would be setting more than one world record, haven't I mentioned that I was among the few authors with the capability to write books in two languages? Now my son of 8 was joining the board!

I knew what I was doing, to give him a sense of purpose and a clear win to feed on. It didn't take long for him to show results.

By the next morning, before leaving for school, he told his mom: « Mommy, I may have difficulties in French, but I am writing books! » and he left for school confident and proud.

I did it, I restored his faith in himself. To me, nothing matters more than confidence. Within a week, I restored his and gave him the mindset of a champion. That was only step one.

By Sunday that week, I had an invitation as a guest speaker on the radio. I knew what effect it might have on William, so I brought him with me. At the beginning, William was glued to his iPad, but as he listened to AM 800 host Terry Kilakos introducing me, he was dying to speak on air too.

Unfortunately for William, that remained a wish. I noticed everything and I wanted him to understand the concept of stardom and consistency.

Later that evening, as I was napping, he went to me and hugged me unexpectedly. « Papa when I'll be a grown-up, I want to be like you... a VIP! »

It took me a few minutes to realize what had just happened! My kid is not just rallying to my footsteps as an author, he wanted to join me in the top 1%!!!

A week ago, I received a warning to slow down. I ignored that friendly warning and speeded up the process enough to celebrate a first world record by scoring a second one... with my kid.

Now William just said boldly that he wanted to join the top 1% by wanting to write more books, by wanting to give interviews and by his resolve to change the world!

I couldn't be more proud of my kid. I couldn't be any more proud of myself as a father! Within a month, I would have removed most of the negative vibes and replaced them with hope and passion. Not just mine, but William's and Tranie's too.

"Give and you shall receive."

I did and I received more than I could have imagined. Listen to your kids, really listen to them. Take actions that will put you out of your comfort zone and inspire them a sense of victory.

You'll be surprised how quickly your children will pick on the vibe, your vibe.

> "Be the difference you want to make.
> That's the only way to grow honestly."
> Dr. Bak Nguyen

From undervalued at school to recipient of a world record, that's a step usually reserved to only a few. The whole time, we ate the same thing, went on with our current life and did not receive any special treatments.

If anything, this put a heavy burden on our daily schedule, but since it was fun, we speeded it up!

It was fun because we both pitched in. I had the experience, the discipline and the structure. William had the energy and the excitement. Together, we fed out of each other hopes and energy.

I have never been as productive as lately. I went out of my challenge of 15/15 exhausted. To score a second record within the next month was not only unexpected, it was unimaginable.

But here we are, almost done. By the time of this writing, we have completed the 6 books and are now about 40% done in our 7th and 8th book: **WE ARE ALL DRAGONS**!

Be open and embrace what today brings. Look up and forward, that's the only path to growth anyway.

This Christmas time is the most memorable ones to each of us, William, Tranie and myself, as a family and as friends... forever!

THE HOUSE OF
DRAGONS

CHAPTER 21
"THE DRAGON HEART"
by Dr. BAK NGUYEN

We are so passed the dragon at this stage! Can we pass the ultimate state? Of course, the ultimate was the beginning. In my previous books about human evolution, I said many times:

> "Our personal legend will only start the day that we are out of our quest of identity."
> Dr. Bak Nguyen

The chicken quest is a quest of identity. For those who choose the super chicken instead of moving into a baby lion, it's the end of the quest of identity too.

Their legend will start and spread among the chicken world. Those who embrace the next level and move into lion babies are still in their quest of identity, only they have pushed their game to something broader than themselves.

Again, some will aim to become a lion king while others will be pushing to fly and to become dragons. The same logic will apply, to the lion king, a lion legend in the animal kingdom. To the dragons, the quest has just begun.

I've spent more than 4 books exploring the concept of the quest of identity, but it is only now that I have the opportunity to find the wording and imagery to clearly state the concept.

"It is all a matter of projection and perspective. The difference is the ripple effect of their influence."
Dr. Bak Nguyen

As you already know, I've started writing children's books with my son to spend some quality time with him. Never would I have imagined that he would be pushing me further and faster along the road.

Already in the lion book, he was giving me advice on how to be happier and to lighten up my heart. That was week 1. By week 2, we were partners, especially after the interviews and podcast.

William became more than motivated, he was impatient to start the next book, the dragon's one. He arrived with a few new ideas as dragons never die and asked me why he never saw a dragon in real life until now?

Was that a silly question? Not if you listen carefully... That gave me the idea of having the dragons changing shape at will, so even if you see a dragon, you don't know it is one! Genius!

From the shape-shifting dragon, that opened the door to even more! The dragon is the beginning, only the beginning of the story... of our personal legend. That was week 3.

The dragon concept allowed me to wrap all that I knew and put it into images that a kid can follow and be attracted to. To be honest, the dragon heart concept would change my writing and imagery forever, even when I wouldn't be writing children's books anymore. It made so much sense!

I am sharing here my unfiltered thoughts with you to disclose that William is really contributing actively to the process. I think all children do so, the chance that I had was to have the presence of mind to listen carefully.

Other than in the chicken book, we both discovered the story as it unfolds before our eyes.

Yesterday, he even said that we are partners, business partners. I laughed, but with careful consideration, I understood his meaning:

"We need each other to grow."
William Bak

I couldn't agree more. I stopped pretending to be an all mighty dad a long time ago. I am still the person who he fears the most though. But between the laughter and the projects, the policeman role has been lesser and lesser. If there is any pride, we crush it with a joke or a friendly slap on the shoulder.

It amuses me to say that I act more like a big brother than a dad to him… at least, that's what I love to tell myself to keep a young heart!

I was fighting my way through life and forced evolution out of me to find out my destiny. I can tell you honestly that before writing with William, I was somehow stuck in the lion phase.

He really gave me my wings and stroke down the gates of both my heart and mind.

Of course, it was consensual, for 9 months I hard reset myself saying YES to most things. But with William's intervention, there was no turning back. A king? No thanks, not for me. I prefer the freedom and the adventure of the dragons!

> "A journey of discovery and of curiosity,
> that's the way of the dragon."
> Dr. Bak Nguyen

With this in mind, all the shoulds and the doubts went silent. I am always teaching my kid and those who want to listen, to treasure gratitude as the primary philosophy of life.

Allow me to express my gratitude to my son, William Bak, who unlocked the upgrades and the next level of evolution to me. Upgrades, unlock and level are all his words.

I dove into his world to connect with him, he touched my heart and mind to transcend my state of mind and the course of my evolution.

"Evolution is a matter of choice and awareness."
Dr. Bak Nguyen

William's merit was to give me more choices to choose from. His questions opened new doors in my mind. And his enthusiasm fuelled my energy for the last month.

8 children's books written within the month of December, the busiest for any CEO. Add on top of that the fact that I was freshly out of a marathon of sprints, writing 15 books within 15 months.
What was truly amazing is that I did it effortlessly, or almost. I even went as far as to make the drawings myself, combining stock images together.

There is a reason why William has his name on the covers, it's because without him, there wouldn't have been no children books at all. Even less a second world record.

I am truly grateful to have said YES. To have listened carefully, to have spent time understanding my kid. And the most beautiful thing of all: I don't even have to teach him what I've learned, he knows and is translating each text from English to French.

Will-I-am? You are, my son! You are inspiration and curiosity within a tender mind. You are wisdom and pure energy within a kind heart.

I usually change for the better the people around me. This time, it is William who made me a better person, more confident and smooth. I am Dr. Bak and my son made me into a dragon.

ACT III
THE LEGEND OF THE
DRAGON HEART

'TO FLY WAS JUST THE BEGINNING...'

by Dr. Bak Nguyen & William Bak

CHAPTER 22
"CHANGING SHAPE"

by Dr. Bak Nguyen & William Bak

You are now
A dragon, papa.
You can fly.

You still have to know
Where to fly to.

Remember that I was the one
Who showed you
How to fly.
Me, the Chicken
That became a Lion,
A baby Lion.

People said
That dragons don't exist.
It's because
Dragons are invisible.

But I can still see you, Papa!
You can see dragons,
You just don't know
They are dragons!

Dragons change shapes
All the time.

> "Try it, Papa!
> Flying was only the beginning!"
> - William Bak

To change shape,
A dragon needs to have both
An open mind,
And an open heart.

He must be **Smart** and **Strong**.
Generous and **Happy**.
But also **Flex-i-ble**.

That word is hard to say, Papa!
It's new, and I know,
New is good.

My dad taught me that word
A while ago: **Flex-i-ble.**
I now understand
Its power.

As I watch my dad,
Saying **YES** to everything...
or almost,

He told me that
It's to become a Lion.
You know what you are good at,
And how to be good at it.

As a dragon,
To be good at something
Is only one shape.

To change shape,
We must be willing
To relearn things,
Even those we are
Good at.

That's called being **Flex-i-ble**.
It's harder than just being
Smart or **Strong**.

It's like you win and then,
You have to play again
But differently.

I am not sure I understand,
But I will learn,
Looking at my dad.
He is the dragon
I am still a baby Lion.

If I want to fly soon,
I must look and learn
How my dad changes shape,
Learn to be **Flex-i-ble.**

When you think
That you know something,
It's just the beginning.

Dragons forever!

CHAPTER 23
"STAY IN CONTROL"

by Dr. Bak Nguyen & William Bak

Now that you are a dragon,
You have much power.

You can fly,
And you can change shapes
As much as you want.

You can make the winds change.
You can make splashes in the lake.
You can even fly around the sun.

And then, as you are flying,
You can decide to change shape
And swim in the ocean
Or walk as a dinosaur
Or sleep under a mountain

> "A dragon can be anything he wants."
> – William Bak

Learn and master the shapes.
That's the homework of the dragons.

But you also have to be in control,
Always and all the time.
This is very important.

If you are not in control,
You might let your anger
Take over.

You might destroy everything.
Because a dragon is so powerful,
It might be impossible
to stop.

Who can stop a dragon?
Another dragon perhaps?
But dragons don't fight
Among themselves,
They know better.

When a dragon is angry,
It spit fire all around
And burn down his home,
His food and his toys
... maybe not his toys
... but his kids' toys.

Hey, what about his kids?
If the house burns down,
Can the chickens
And the baby lions get out?

If you are a dragon,
You must be in control
All the time.

That's why we must train hard
Before we become dragons.

"No one is born with a dragon heart.
A dragon heart is earned."
- William Bak

A chicken that's not in control
Is just a crazy chicken!
Sometimes, a headless chicken.

A Lion that loses control
Can be dangerous.

But a dragon,
If he loses control,
He is more than dangerous.

He becomes a monster
Worse than in your
Nightmares!

That's not good papa!
What happens
If you stay a monster?

I'm scared Papa!
I don't want to lose you!
Promise me to never become
A monster.

Promise me to stay in control,
Always and forever.

So you can keep changing shape
And fly as a dragon,
As a king in the sky.
Wait for me,
I am coming soon to race you
And beat you!

I'm just kidding...
But I'm coming

Dragons forever!

CHAPTER 24
"FEAR WILL DISAPPEAR WITH ACTION"

by Dr. Bak Nguyen & William Bak

As powerful as a dragon can be,
A dragon has fears too.

But a dragon does not let
His fear control him.
He makes something
Out of his fears.

"He knows that fear cannot hurt him. Fear can only scare him."
- William Bak

To be scared is bad enough,
Because when you have bad dreams,
You can't sleep.

If you can't sleep,
You are weak
And angry
Most of the time.

> "Fear will turn a dragon into a monster."
> - William Bak

This is why fear is the most
Dangerous thing
For a dragon.

He knows that it is there
And as soon as he sees it,
He has to do something with it,
With his fear.

I know that my dad
Is always running away
From fear.

He runs so fast
That fear is left far behind.
That is how he learned to fly!

Another time,
I saw him laugh so hard at fear,
That he scared fear away…

That's how he learned
To sing and tell jokes.
That's my favourite shape of him,
When he tells jokes
And makes everyone laugh.

The last time,
I saw him face fear,
He charged head down
And fear disappeared
Like thin air.

That's the power of the dragon,
To be in action.

> "Every time a dragon takes action,
> fear will disappear into thin air."
> - William Bak

My dad said that fear is good.
It forced him to take action
And to learn new shapes.

Without fear,
He might get stuck with
Just one or two shapes.

Even if he said that fear is good,
I don't like fear.
So I run away too.
Wait a minute,
That's how I will learn
To fly...

Dragons forever!

CHAPTER 25
"HOW MANY DRAGONS ARE OUT THERE?"

by Dr. Bak Nguyen & William Bak

No one knows
How many dragons
Are out there.
Because no one can see
What they really are.

What I do know
Is that dragons recognize
Each other by closing
Their eyes.

> "Dragons don't see each other,
> they feel each other."
> - William Bak

They see with their hearts.
That's the only way
To recognize a dragon.

With their heart, they also feel
Lions and chickens too.

Until you can see
With the eyes of your heart,
You are not a dragon yet.

> "With the eyes of the heart, dragons see everything!"
> – William Bak

Since dragons see with their heart,
They are also taking
The shape of their **emotions**.

Each emotion they feel,
They take that shape
For a little while.

That's why they must stay
In control of their emotions
To master their shapes.

That's also how
They have so many shapes.
It is called **trans-cen-dence**
Another new word.

*"Flex-i-ble first and then,
trans-cen-dence is the
next new word."*
- William Bak

Each single emotion
Has a different shape
And different powers.

Happiness for example,
Will make a dragon fly.
Happiness is light and contagious,
It will make dragons come together.

And when two dragons
Or more come together,

It's like fireworks!
Magic is in the air!

Dragons forever!

CHAPTER 26
"FROM SADNESS WILL COME JOY"

by Dr. Bak Nguyen & William Bak

Sadness will make
A dragon lose his wings.
It will make a dragon
Cry so much.

It will swim in his own tears.
Every time a dragon cries,
A new lake is born.

The dragon is still very powerful.
Swimming lonely in his bubble,
The new lake.

It is a good thing that he cried.
Because once the sadness is out,
He might change shape again
And fly away.

If he didn't cry,
The sadness would never
Go away.

This is one of the main things
That he has to change
To transform from
A lion into a dragon.

After a dragon cries,
His tears become a lake.

Once he flies away,
The lake becomes
A great place of joy
And happiness
To the chicken and lions.

"From sadness, will come joy
if you are a dragon."
- William Bak

A chicken is taught
To stop crying
To become a lion.

When a chicken cries,
He is asking for help
Or he is saying
That he is not happy.

He is not doing much.
No lake will come from his tears,
Even if he cries forever...

A lion is taught
Never to cry
Like a chicken.

Since a lion takes action,
He doesn't have the time
To say that he is not happy.

A lion goes to find his own happiness.
He needs to find something
To fight the sadness.

He has no time to cry.
A lion must run pretty far
To escape sadness.

A dragon just needs
To let the tears out
To turn sadness into joy.
Maybe not his own,
But at least, the joy
Of others.

A dragon is trained
To embrace his tears.
Only he must stay
In control, always.

In control enough
To be the power of the tears
Until they become something else.
A dragon is not fighting his tears,
They were just his fears.

"A dragon uses the power of his tears to be more powerful."

— William Bak

Remember that a dragon
Was once a chicken.
The heart of the dragon
Is still the same little heart
Which grew into a lion heart.

It got bigger and lighter,
Enough to fly
And one minute later,
Flexible enough to swim.

For a dragon, to fly in the waves
Or to swim with the clouds
Are two of the same things.

Actually, the heart of the dragon
Is the heart of the lion,
But so open
That it has no doors.

Dragons forever!

CHAPTER 27
"THE CHICKEN BRAIN"

by Dr. Bak Nguyen & William Bak

The secret of the dragons
Is the chicken brain.
All dragons were
Chickens once.

The chicken may be small,
But he learns fast.
As he becomes bigger
And as he grows
Into a lion.

It's hard to keep up
With his learning speed.

"As a dragon, every time he feels,
he has to master a new shape."
- William Bak

Unlearning everything he knew
From the last shape
To embrace the new one
Is the difficult part.

The more he can empty
Both his mind and heart,
The more new powers
he will learn.

> "Once he masters the new shape,
> a new emotion will come."
> - William Bak

And the dragon will
Unlearn to learn again.
All dragons do that.

Some are faster than others
They are almighty and powerful.

> "Those who master more shapes
> have more fun, that's all."
> - William Bak

The secret of learning a new shape
Is the chicken brain.

If a dragon can keep
His chicken brain,
That's the most open brain
And the fastest way
To learn new things.

A chicken brain with a lion heart.
The dragon will have to control
And to feel only one emotion.

One at a time
In order to master
The new shape.

The dragon needs the power to focus.
That's what will give time to the dragon
To master its new shape.

So a dragon
Is not really a new animal.
He is a chicken brain
with a lion heart.

As he flies and changes shape,
He is now a dragon heart,
A force of Nature
Breeding life.

Dragons forever!

CHAPTER 28
"DRAGONS DON'T FIGHT AMONG THEMSELVES"

by Dr. Bak Nguyen & William Bak

Dragons do not fight.
They are forces of Nature.
Sometimes, they clash by accident
But they do not fight.

Dragons don't like to fight each other.
Because they are all
brothers and sisters.

They have the same blood,
The same training
And no one understands them better
Than another dragon.

Chickens fight
Among themselves
All the time.

Lions, when they do,
They can hurt each other
Badly.

> "Dragons, if they fight,
> they will destroy the whole world!"
> – William Bak

The power of the dragon
Is not to be tested.
The power of the dragon
Is to be forever.
To transcend
Shapes and time.

Since the fun of the dragon
Is to master new shapes,
They have to learn
From the other dragons.

They know that sharing
Makes them more powerful!
They are not looking to be the best,
But to have fun.

They want to learn new shapes.
They have no interest
In fighting each other.

> "There is zero fun in fighting!"
> - William Bak

Lions and chickens fight
Not dragons.
They have the power
To kill and to destroy,
But that's no fun at all!

For a dragon, to fly
He must be light.
The only way to be light
Is to have fun
And to be happy!

Dragons forever!

CHAPTER 29
"THE CIRCLE OF THE DRAGON"

by Dr. Bak Nguyen & William Bak

They were here
When the dinosaurs
Walked the earth.

They were here
When the knights
Of the round table
Were superstars.

Dragons met with the Vikings.
Dragons are even on TV,
When you know what to look for.

It takes much time
And training to become
a dragon.

And even more efforts
To keep learning new shapes
To be invisible.

But the real power of the dragon
Is to live forever!

"Dragons can die only if they lose a fight to another force of Nature."
— William Bak

That's why they avoid fighting each other.
Even when they disagree,
Dragons will prefer to leave
Than to fight.

If they fight,
One of them
Will die.

And the other,
Even if he wins,
May not survive
Either.

If he does,
He will be left very weak,
Weaker than a super chicken.

"Dragons are more than flying lions!"
- William Bak

Because they do not fight each other,
Dragons are powerful.
They are forces of Nature
Nature is not about fighting.
Nature is about living.

A dragon is a force of Life
He feels the emotions.
Emotions that are the colors
Of the world.

That's what makes
The world so beautiful!

Dragons can spit fire,
But gently,
Only to warm up the world.
To chase winter away
In Spring time.

Dragons are the guardians of Life.
They remind all of us that we are part
Of something bigger.

Even their powers are found
When they keep unlearning
To learn again.

From little to open,
From open to growing
From growing to powerful.

> "And from powerful to little again.
> That's the circle of dragons."
> – William Bak

When a dragon is tired,
He goes under a mountain
To sleep.

Maybe for years until he wakes up
To fly again in a different shape,
In a different time
As a dragon,

Breathing life and wisdom.
Not fire.

Dragons forever!

CHAPTER 30
"... JUST LIKE IN THE BEGINNING..."

by Dr. Bak Nguyen & William Bak

A year ago, I first discovered
That I was a chicken heart.
Since then, I've grown much.
I've kept my mind open to learn
And to grow into a lion heart.

As I wrote those books,
I helped my dad empty his heart
So he can finally grow
Into a dragon heart
And fly away.

Flying was only the first step.

Then, we both discovered
How dragons can change shapes
And be invisible.

Even live forever,
Thanks to their chicken brains...
And their lion hearts.

The more you grow,
The more Big and Little
Are the same.

The chicken is weaker than the lion.
The lion is weaker than the dragon.
But to grow, the lion got help
from the chicken.
And the dragon has to use
Their chicken brains...

> "We are all important.
> To each its appropriate timing"
> – William Bak

I've learned two new words
Flex-i-ble and **Trans-cen-dence**
There is a third one to add
Hu-mili-ty

That means that
We are all important.
No matter our size,
We just need to know
Our strengths to be,
Just be.

The only real weakness
Is to get stuck
A a super chicken,
A lion king
Or a dragon monster

> "Power is within change."
> – William Bak

If you are stuck
By a closed mind or heart,
You slowly lose your powers,
Either as a chicken,
A lion or a dragon.

> "A heart, that's the constant of the legends."
> – William Bak

The heart is the legend!
Chicken to dragon,
The heart is what matters.
The heart and the openness.

This is my secret
And I share it with you.
Wishing that we will all
Become dragons one day
So we will stop fighting
Each other.

Dragons forever!

CHAPTER 31
"THE DRAGON'S JOURNEY"
by Dr. BAK NGUYEN

Each of the books has a special standing and meaning to me. As the Chicken Heart was the beginning of something new, an adventure that took over a year to launch, it allowed William and I to find each other.

The Chicken Heart is my book, if I can speak in that sense. It was me trying to get William into my world of thoughts and of human behaviours. I threw at him concepts and used his words and logic to write the legend.

If the Chicken Heart was mine, the Lion Heart is definitely his, from the very beginning, he was throwing back at me ways for me to be happier.

To have the Chicken helping the Lion grow was my idea, but I didn't have to reach really far, I just looked at him and the enthusiasm he had to share back.

As I told you, this year was a rocky year with Tranie. I am finally through with my Midlife crisis and we did fight more than once. William heard bits and pieces and was affected by our fights.

He was very clever on the way to communicate his fears and emotions. The Lion Heart gave him a legitimate channel in which he could express, not his opinion, bu his advice to cate for his parents.

To any grown up, this is cute. To a father, this is a blow to the heart. A good blow, but still, a big one. Where does it stop, that bond of love between father and son? I wasn't ashamed that my kid was teaching me, I was amazed and grateful.

> "I gave into it without holding back, empowering William to speak with confidence."
> Dr. Bak Nguyen

This is where the magic happened. William was now more than a beneficiary, he was recognized as a full member of the clan, our clan. Until then, he loved me because I was his dad, because I was his every day Santa, because I was the figure of authority.

Since the Lion Heart, he was looking forward to be in my presence and to share time with me. Not just playing with me, he was also looking to sit down and talk with me.

After his interviews, he somehow focused on my status. What he called work and being busy before looking at me, he now craved for.

To see him walking tall getting to school and to telling, not to his friends, but to other adults that he wrote books was simply beautiful to look at. And nothing happened in vain.

I got inspired from his vibe to push myself, once again, scoring in the unknown. You see, I can write. I only need to find the right structure first and then, understand the themes. But a children's book required more than just words.

It needs strong and original concepts, even that was okay. The void concerned the imagery... And in that field, I had no clue nor talent. Or so I thought.

I remembered clearly that last year, this is where I had gotten stuck, trying to find the imagery first in order to feed my inspiration. Now, I had 2/3 of the trilogy of Legends written, but still no illustrations. I reached out to my friends and teams and they started looking for the right people.

> "Have I told you that I do not wait? I have a distorted notion of time to be more precise."
> Dr. Bak Nguyen

I didn't want to sit on my hands and wait. Christmas was coming and to be fair, it would be very hard to find artists that could be interviewed, passed the selection process, understanding the feeling that I was looking for and to deliver before the end of the year. In my everyday life, I am a CEO, I know all too well the process of delegation.

I couldn't just go on and write the last tome, the Dragon Heart since William was in the middle of his tests and I needed to sit down with him before I could draw the chapters and bring words to life.

*"I hate to wait. There is no hope for me there.
I can prepare though."*
Dr. Bak Nguyen

While « *waiting* » for William and for people to come back at me, I started searching within my resources, themes and images that would point the artists in the right direction.

I spent a weekend searching and sorting royalty free cartoon images. I bought a few hundreds and started putting them together. Within 3 days, I had the 22 finished images needed for the whole trilogy. I even changed the cover of the Lion Heart.

"I didn't want to do the job. I was simply keeping my momentum going… on the back burner…"
Dr. Bak Nguyen

The imagery brought magic into our adventure. To William it was the third proof that he was making books. The first one was the words he saw with his name signed.

The second was the interviews as he had the chance to talk about his experience. The third was to hold the PDF version on his iPad scrolling through his books, with the imagery. These were now real children books, in colour!

The excitement was at an all time high. We were now two weeks and a half into the production and I wanted to get it over with before Christmas. We had about a week before the deadline.

It was also clear to me that I would be pushing for a second world record, writing 6 children books with my co-author of 8, within a month.

We had much time to think about the Chicken Heart. The Lion Heart was William's reaction to our life. But the Dragon Heart, what would this book be about? Neither of us had a clear view on it.

We knew that a flying lion would turn into a dragon. That was an ultimate goal, to fly! What then? In his interview, William said

"If you want something, do not wait for anything.
Do it! Make your dreams come true."
William Bak

Truth... why is it that the dragons are not real in our everyday life? By discussing with him one evening, he inspired the idea that dragons are invisible. I wanted to teach him the concept of being flexible.

"Invisible and flexible were the smash up
of our geniuses."
Dr. Bak Nguyen and William Bak

We arrived with the idea that dragons can change shapes. Flying was only the beginning. But first they need to master new shape, to unlearn what they knew to learn again.

That's how dragons are invisible, we see them, but we don't know that we are looking at a dragon! And since they keep learning, they stay young forever! It was magical! From that point on, the chapters were written almost by themselves.

I was still using the wording of an 8 year-old, but I took over from where I left, finishing **FORCES OF NATURE**, my 15th book. The Dragon is more than a children book, it is my legacy and the whole of my views on human evolution and philosophy.

Being forced to use the wording of an 8 year-old was pretty restrictive and a blessing at the same time. It forced me to sort out my ideas and my concepts.

I am particularly proud of Dragon Heart. I used William's imagination and gave it meaning and depth. I refined the concept to the point where he thinks that the ideas are all his.

Did I tell you that I am lazy? Now, I don't even have to teach him nor to convince him anymore, he wrote the book!

Even the decision to put his name first in the French version gave meaning to the entire process, since he had to translate every single word of our English manuscript. Of course, I did help and correct the rhetoric.

> "If anything, William gave me my wings, as a dragon."
> Dr. Bak Nguyen

This is not a figure of speech. It is as real as it can be. We wrapped the Trilogy of the Legends in both languages, French and English, came out with all of the imagery within a little more than 3 weeks. By the 23 in the morning, we were done before noon.

I am fast writing and producing, but never has it been as easy and as smooth, producing as much! This trilogy you are holding is not a fragment of our imagination to neither William nor me.

It is the story of our bond together, of the evolution of a father-son relationship, now partnership.

If this is the last book of the Trilogy, I am glad that I gave William the best of myself for this Christmas, 6 books, a Guinness Record, Confidence and a Magic Bond.

I truly hope that you have enjoyed the journey as much I we had.

Yours.
Dr. Bak Nguyen

CHAPTER 32
"INFINITY"
by Dr. BAK NGUYEN

As planned, the writing of Dragon Heart took a week. We went through a last sprint on Sunday morning, the 23rd to translate the last four chapters in French.

William had gained much in confidence and vocabulary since the beginning of this endeavour, a few weeks ago.

Writing a trilogy in a short while, the danger is to run out of ideas or to start repeating ourselves. It wasn't the case here. Both energy and inspiration were at their peak.

As fatigue started to settle in, the motivation to finish before Christmas with a second world record pushed me forward. And William, after the interviews and podcast, he was actively looking forward for more!

What amazed me is that has found the whole process smooth and easy. Our two first books had 7 chapters each plus a conclusion. For the Dragon Heart, I pushed to 8 chapters, explaining to him the significance of the number 8 in Asian culture, the 8 of the dragon.

8 is infinite. Chinese people believe that 8 is not just a lucky number, it is the sign of the dragon, a sign of infinite wisdom, power and wealth. Not that I care

much about the faith and folklore, but I wanted to use the infinite dragon logo for the book...

So we wrote eight chapters for the last book of our trilogy. Eight chapters plus conclusion. In the end, all it took was a an extra hour to fulfill the dragon's destiny.

> "Be careful what you wish for, especially around me!"
> Dr. Bak Nguyen

This is a joke I often make around as a warning. It is both a joke and a warning all at once. People within my close entourage have grown aware and are taking the warning very seriously since words rarely remain words for a long time in my presence...

This time, it was me who got trapped. I was willing to commit for a trilogy, not completely sure how to write it nor to know where it would go.

To have scored a second world record three weeks after the first one was a great surprise! To be a hero to my kid who had now joined the producers and thinkers of this world without any pressure from my part was a much welcomed bonus.

To have strengthened his confidence from a failure at school to a prodigy in both French and English wasn't surely part of even my wildest dreams. By Christmas this year, I could use the brake and celebrate two well deserved victories.

> "Papa, I want to do more!"
> William Bak

I couldn't believe my ears. We just finished writing 6 books, the last chapters were in this morning and the kid already wanted more! He wanted to know how dragons would transform...

It was all just a big joke... but since it was Christmas time and William didn't ask for anything for Christmas, why not? I still had the right to a few hundred images royalty free.

While I was waiting for his mom to get prepared and to shop, I played around with the computer and within an hour and a half, compiled et created 10 new images for the two next books, if there would be any.

I loved the enthusiasm and was so proud of my son joining in the top 1% and the leader's class that I did the unthinkable.

I compiled the structure and the images for a fourth book: **WE ARE ALL DRAGONS**, telling the story of all the other animals wanting to have a chance to evolve into dragon hearts too.

To be honest, I wanted to empower William and his Confidence, but it wasn't on the table to be writing and finishing this one before the end of the month. We were leaving for a cruise in less than 2 days for the rest of the year...

> "But Papa, you said that 8 is the infinite number?"
> William Bak

He got me corner. He was right! 6 is a world record and a statement to the world. 8 would be a statement to the universe. I started to give it some serious thoughts.

Tranie, as she heard of the foolishness, was absolutely against the idea! She planned so hard to reserve the trip and to get me on board.

She didn't want to mortgage our end of the year's trip with a childish impossible challenge.

> "But honey, the kid is right, it would be a great statement to make!"
> Dr. Bak Nguyen

That evening, I had to pass by the office to help a friend in need of dentistry... yes, I am still a doctor. I brought William in with me.

He patiently waited for me to finish the treatment and we went up to my CEO's office where I have a whole white wall on which we could plan the last book.

You see, that white wall in my office was the best investment I made, we drew so many plans to change the world within a few months, that it became a privilege to be seated in my office and to experience one of my white wall experiences.

I wanted to treat William as a VIP, giving him the same consideration I gave to my most trusted partners.

He adored the process and we arrived with a master plan within 2 hours of board meeting. He was fuelled and excited and so was I!

We had family events scheduled within the next two days and by the 26th, in the early morning, we would be driving to New York city to catch our cruise to Miami and the Bahamas.

I knew that on the cruise, I might have a chance to write, but that would be by the 28th. I wouldn't have much time to write and would again be squeezed by impossible deadlines... Tranie had a very good point! But so did William.

> "To give him infinity and a world record, that would be a hell of a Christmas gift!"
> Dr. Bak Nguyen

I went online and announced the completion of **Dragon Heart**. In the same post, I slipped in the mention that we would be trying to add 2 other books to the mix: **WE ARE ALL DRAGONS**, both in French and English. That was enough to me to get me committed.

I had ups and downs this year, both in business and in my love life. I was determined to cross the finishing line with a big blow, a legendary victory! To beat my own new world record!

That's the way of the dragon! To unlearn in order to learn again and to be reborn into a new shape! I could easily sit on my last victory writing 6 children's books within a month...

William made the bet for me! To have two other books, with a brand new concept and to have it done within about a week, once again. But this week was the Christmas holidays and the End of the year trip.

Am I a dragon or not? It seems that I am one. Despite my most logic self and the love of Tranie, I went all in with William...

Oh, I forgot to tell you that I also needed to drive to New York! That would also drain a portion of the available time and energy...

Merry Christmas!

ACT IV
WE ARE ALL
DRAGONS

"THE MORE SHAPES A DRAGON MASTERS, THE MORE THE FUN"
by Dr. Bak Nguyen & William Bak

CHAPTER 33
THE SHARK
MASTER CONTROL

BY DR. BAK NGUYEN & WILLIAM BAK

Since there are so many dragon shapes,
There is more than one way to reach
That level of evolution.

I am a shark, and I have bad press.
Just like anyone else,
I feed when I am hungry.

But every time
I feed, I am a monster!

Those pointing their fingers at me
Feed themselves too
With smaller living creatures!

"Life is not about fairness. It's about give and take."
— William Bak

It hurts my feelings
But again, I am hungry
So I eat those pointing
Their fingers at me.

And then, the silence is a great relief.
The silence is a great reward,
But the whispering never really stops.

This drives me crazy
When I am among
My friends, the other sharks.
We fight and compete
Against each other.

There is much jealousy
And gossip there too.
I grew tired of the word.

That's why I left to hunt on my own.
And then, as I was alone
I started hearing the talks
Of the other fishes.

One day, I heard about a dragon.
It got me curious.
A lonely powerful creature

Which commands
The respect of Nature.

Hey, I fit the description
Except that I command fear.

The better I become,
The more fearful they get
Even if they are not
On my menu.

"We are what we eat!"

I don't want to become any of them.
Since I do not want to gossip.
I will be sick eating junk food all the time
But again, that's all I know.

I must resist my urges
To eat the usual fishes.
As soon as I see one
Or as soon as I smell one.

"If I can resist my urges I will change"
- William Bak

I need the time to select
My next meal
Something new…

They say that to grow,
One must have an open mind
By resisting, I am forcing myself
To try the new, the undiscovered.

> "Since I am what I eat, I will be different, I will change."
> - William Bak

But first, I need to be in control.
I need to resist my urges
Always in control,
Of the animal inside

I will still eat,
I will still grow,
I will still reign over the sea
But in my terms,
Not my food's terms.

Who knows,
The dragon they are talking about
Is my shadow.
I know, and I just don't care

I am a shark,
You can call me
Whatever you want,
That won't stop me
From being strong,
And powerful,
In control of my fate.

The key is to resist
And master control.

I am a shark,
Shadow of the dragon.

CHAPTER 34
THE PANDA
MASTER HARMONY

BY DR. BAK NGUYEN & WILLIAM BAK

I am a Panda
I am known
For my peaceful attitude

I can eat meat
But I choose to eat
Bamboo instead.

Because I like the taste
And because there is so much
Bamboo all around.

I do not disturb
Much of the world
Nor does it disturb me.

> "I live and let live, that's my mantra.
> Until now, I had a great Life."
> - Dr. Bak Nguyen

If needed, I can defend myself.
If you push me
There is still a bear inside
Hidden somewhere.

But I love myself better
Peaceful and relaxed
I am lazy
I am not seeking
To save the world.

> "I am seeking to leave the world untouched
> by my presence. It's all about give and take."
> - Dr. Bak Nguyen

Since I am lazy
I try to take
As least as possible
So I will not have
To give back that much.

By my shy presence in the world,
I'll leave my footprint
On almost nothing,
Since the bamboo replenishes
Faster than I can eat them.

I live a life of Abundance
Because I share my forest,
Because I do not fight,
Because I sleep
And eat peacefully.

I am no dragon,
I am too lazy
To be a dragon
Saving the world.

Wait a minute,
That's no dragon,
To save the world,
That's a lion talking!

To prove themselves,
Lions aim to be heroes.
Dragons are forces of Nature
Parts of the elements.

I heard that Dragons live forever!
And can change shape
With their emotions.

If I didn't know better,
I must have been
A dragon in my past life.

Since I am one with Nature,
Part of the Elements,
Living in harmony,
With both Nature
And the world.
I am a Panda!

I do not want to become
Anything else than myself.
I love my Life.

If you have the chance
To experience my destiny
You too, will understand
The wisdom of being me,
Of being lazy.

"I am lazy since I've reached harmony..."
- Dr. Bak Nguyen

The Life of a Panda
Is not for everyone
Some will require more action
And purpose to be happy.

I don't.
I am happy as is.

I know that tomorrow
May be different
I've lived long enough
To adapt myself.
But until the problem presents itself,
There is no problem!

I am a Panda
This is my wisdom
The ultimate state of a dragon
To rest harmoniously.

CHAPTER 35
THE RHINO
MASTER PATIENCE

BY DR. BAK NGUYEN & WILLIAM BAK

I am a Rhino
I too, have
A bad reputation.

They say it's about my temper!
If you provoke me
And you live to tell the tale,
You won't be telling
A great story!

Of course I would have
A bad reputation!
That's how you thank me
For sparing your life?

"What an ungrateful world."
- William Bak

I learned that years ago,
As my friends underwent
The natural training of Rhinos.

We have mastered
The art of focusing.
We are feared
Even when we are calm.

From the outside,
We look relaxed.
But inside,
We are summering
The energy in our palm.

Just like sunlight
Can be focused within a beam
And burn away a forest,
We have the power to harness
Energy to destroy
A wall within a single blow.

Do not provoke a Rhino
That's a friendly advice.

But I want to do more
What more can I achieve
With focus and patience?

"Patience doesn't mean to wait."
— Dr. Bak Nguyen

Then, I met that chicken
Talking about growing into a lion...
And then flying away as a dragon...
I never heard something
That distasteful!

No chicken can fly,
No lion is a dragon.
And a lion with feathers
Is an error of nature!

I am bored with my own life,
I could use a change too.
I have the power to destroy.
What about the power to build?

I've already mastered patience
And the art of focusing
I just need a plan
A purpose to concentrate
My energy.

"Anything of worth required patience."
— William Bak I too will grow into a dragon

Just because I can be more
Than a Rhino
Charging in head down.

This time, I will master the purpose
To build something I can be proud of.

Not to show the others
Since they will always
Find something bad to say.
I will build to be proud of myself.

If the others can enjoy it,
That's great for them.
It won't change a thing for me
I just need a purpose…

Life can be ironic
That means that
Life will give you
What you dislike
The most…

That happened to me the day
I discovered that
The most powerful Purpose
Is to care about others.

Yes, those others
Who were laughing
At me.

But what are my choices?
To keep destroying?
To build thing with no purpose?
Or to care about things
That might not last?

Anything of worth takes time.
It took me years to understand
The dragon sleeping in me.

To open my mind and heart,
To listen to the needs of others.
And to recognize my purpose.
But with time, I finally understood.

Today I am a builder,
I still charge head down
In the pursuit of my fate
Not my food nor my enemy.

"I might not fly, but I might last forever, as long as my purpose serves the many."
- Dr. Bak Nguyen

I am a Rhino,
Shadow of a dragon.

CHAPTER 36
THE HIPPO
MASTER DREAMS

BY DR. BAK NGUYEN & WILLIAM BAK

Hi, I am a Hippo,
Contrary to many
Of my friends here,
I have good press.

I eat when I am hungry
I cry out when I am angry
It's natural,
It's the course of Life

Even if I am
A respected size animal
I love delicacy and finesse
Above all, I live to travel
And to see the world.

I may not fly
But I can surely
Walk the miles.

I follow the mood
And the winds,
To discover earth's
True beauties.

I am a lady,
And I like to act as one.
I keep my temper under control,
And my urges for myself.

The only thing I gave into
Are my dreams.

Those dreams pushing me
To embrace the day
Those dreams forcing me
To say "YES"
To most things.

"We don't know until we try."
- William Bak

Of course, like anything else
Some will be of bad taste
Some will be great surprises
The only way to know,
You need to try.

That's what travelling taught me
To embrace the possibilities
To try the different food
To see the colors
And to tastes the world.

> "Beauty is in the multitude.
> Grown ups call it diversity."
> - William Bak

I started with one dream,
To travel and met with people.

I grew my dreams too
I understood that dreams are maps
Of what's to come.

I can either follow someone else's map
Or to draw my own.
Why not do both?
We don't know until we've tried,
Right?

After having seen
Part of the world,
I've learned
One thing for sure.

No matter whose dream it is
For as long as I keep travelling
And discovering new tastes
I am happy. I am in.

The worst would be to settle down,
Waiting for dreams to pass you by.
There is just too much to see
To waste one single day
Sitting and waiting.

I am no dragon,
I am a lady
A lady Hippo
Who likes to travel.

Since I travelled that much
I keep my heart
Young and open.

Maybe that's what
The chicken is calling
A dragon heart.

Hey, if that could help me fly
And travel more,
I am all in.

Until I learn to fly,
I will be flying
With my imagination,
Visiting the panoramas
And the fields.

Never stop moving
Living and leaving forever...
For better, worse...
For the new.

You might not recognize
A dragon when you see one.
Me, you'll see me everywhere!
So come and say hi!

I am a Hippo,
A lady, not a dragon,
But still,
I will stay young forever!

CHAPTER 37
THE MONKEY
MASTER HUMILITY

BY DR. BAK NGUYEN & WILLIAM BAK

I am a star,
An acclaimed comedian,
And a rockstar,
Dancing and singing
I am also a Monkey.

I was born smart
I was gifted
With many skills.

I can connect
Easily with people
They love me,
They adore me.

Some hate me.
Anyway, they all remember me,
The Monkey!

I was a King once,
Or twice…

It's boring to be King!
I prefer to be happy.
Life is a big joke to me.

That's how I make people laugh.
That's how I am happy
All the time.

But that's not all true.

By default, I am happy
But in truth, I hide my emotions
Behind the laughters
And the smiles.

I know I am good,
And better than most.
I am still no lion
Nor dragon.
Do I need to become one?

"To each its own destiny."

My forefathers were
King Kong and the Monkey King.
They all suffered
Much for being King.

I know better,
Keep the kingship for yourself,
A rockstar is a better Life!

> "At least as a rockstar,
> I can let my emotions flow freely."
> - Dr. Bak Nguyen

Like the Hippo,
I live my Life to be happy
Since I was born happy
What should I master more?
Humility.

> "Humility is the ability to recognize and to respect what we are, and stop pretending to be what we are not."
> - Dr. Bak Nguyen

I learned that
Looking at the Kings.
And the monkeys
In my clan.

I will make people laugh.
I will make people love me.
I will protect my family.
I am proud to be a Monkey!

I have no crown
But I still live like a King!
Free and happy.

Actually,
I live better than a King
Since freedom and happiness
Are no King's menu.

And dragons?
I can make them laugh.
I can entertain them
When they are bored.
I can ride on their back
Once we are friends.

I too, am lazy.
But I am too energized
To be a Panda.

I need to have fun
And to make noise.
I play my strengths
And respect what nature
Intended for me.

> "To project is not the same than to pretend. To project is to say what will be. To pretend is to say what is not and will never be."
> - Dr. Bak Nguyen

I stop pretending
To be what I am not.
I keep embracing
What I am.

I still want to evolve
To be better,
Stronger and smarter.

I might not fly as a dragon,
I am a Monkey!

I can manage a flight
If and when I need a ride,
I am a Monkey

And dragons are my friends.

CHAPTER 38
THE PIG
MASTER GRATITUDE

BY DR. BAK NGUYEN & WILLIAM BAK

I am a pig
My life was made easy
To eat, to bathe in mud
And one day,
To be eaten.

I made peace with that.
Everyone has to die someday
Of something.
That's what they say.

Since they will eat me,
I eat everything
That I can get my teeth on.
Like most of my friends,
I grew fat Bored
And ungrateful.

Until one day, I met a chicken.
He too was to be eaten.

His fate was even worst than mine,
Since from his hatching
He had to survive
From the egg to the chicken.

I felt better for a little while.
Until I noticed
The hope he held
Within his heart.

The chicken was talking about growing,
About lions,
About flying one day,
About dragons.

To do so,
He needed to open up
To grow and to hope.

Growing I knew
Hoping? Nope!

I was eating
And waiting to be eaten
Where is the hope in that?

But the chicken
Found a way
To grow into a lion.

Nobody, in their right mind
Will try to eat a lion!
The chicken never focused
On his fate.

He was making up
His own destiny.
And some really grew
Into lions and dragons.

As a pig,
I want the hope too.
I want to be grateful,
So I can see beyond
The fate intended for me,
And make my own.

I started to appreciate
Everything given to me.
I decided to make
The most out of it.

They feed me,
I say thank you.

They give me time,
So I start to train.
To run fast,
Even in the mud.

I even play with them
Having them chasing me,
So I could run faster.

> "For as long as I am grateful,
> I have time to train to be better."
> – William Bak

I will train until the day
They won't be able to catch me
Anymore.

Maybe that day,
I will have gained
My freedom.

Or at least, earned their respect
As a racing pig,
A champion.

"Make leverage of your liabilities!"
— Dr. Bak Nguyen

Is a champion a dragon?
I don't know,
But if I start
By being a champion first,
Then, let's find out
What will come next!

I am a pig
And I am training
To fly away.

CHAPTER 39
THE ELEPHANT
MASTER AWARENESS

BY DR. BAK NGUYEN & WILLIAM BAK

I am an Elephant,
People have mixed
Feelings about me.

Some consider me
A war machine.
Others, a clumsy big animal,
And some, a divinity.

I am all of the above.
I am a kind heart,
I usually try to please.

What's hurtful is that
People misunderstand me.

I am not slow,
I am careful.

I am a big guy,
That I know.

I slow down,
To make sure
I am not crushing
Anyone around.
I am aware.

I am not dumb,
I try to please.
That's how they tricked me
Into a war machine.

I can be scary and fearless
All I do is to try to please
Until I realize
That I was tricked,
Not loved.

About being a divinity,
Those things come and go.
As trend changes Ego,
I've learned
To always be careful
Of those who flatter.

I am no fool,
I saw the dinosaurs
Disappear.

The reason why I am so aware
Is because every time you think you're on top,
Something will simply knock you down!
That's why dinosaurs are no more.

Life runs everywhere.
Size does not matter.
Life is life.
That's my kindness
To the world.

CHAPTER 40
THE FOX
MASTER IMAGINATION

BY DR. BAK NGUYEN & WILLIAM BAK

I am a Fox
I am known
To be smart.

Not always the best kind
Of smartness, but smart.
I'll take that.

To be smart is not enough.
I've never been the King of anything.
The best I've been recognized for
Is to trick a raven for its meal.

I am so much more than this!
But you see, in Life
There is no complain's department.
I learned this a long time ago!

Not that I care about being King,
But it's nice to have the option.

I am a Fox,
A Dragon in the making
And that, no ones
Know about my ambition.
No one cares.

To be a dragon and to live forever,
I still need to find out how.
Since the others have found ways
I need to up my game,
Now.

It's not about competing,
But about not being
Left behind.

For years, that kept me going
Until I understood that I had
The wrong Mindset.

I do not want
To become a dragon.
I only want to matter.

For some, they will be
Satisfied as lions.
For me, it's about being remembered,
For my place among others.

I saw Rhino building,
I saw chicken flying,
I saw lion swimming,
What can a Fox do?

> "With imagination and patience,
> all you need is a purpose to matter."
> – William Bak

That's what missing, Imagination.
That's how I got bad press!
Words and imagination spreading
That's my way out of the nest.

I will use my words and imagination
To paint a new reality,
One where we all have a chance to matter.
One where each of us meets their destiny.

All it will take,
Is for me to believe

In my words and my potential,
Because by New Year's Eve,
Everyone has a chance
To start over.

I am a Fox,
But even dragons
Will need me,
Since I will get them
Out of their box,
To fly, climb and surf
Over the sea.

I am making dragons
Thanks to my words
And imagination.

If they believe it
They will dance on the beat
Of their own Reality.

> "I do not take no for an answer!"
> – William Bak

That's how I will fly with them.
From my words and fate,

I will empower each of them.

I will help them find their inner power
And originate a unique
Tale of their own.

> "No is just the beginning of a great adventure."
> - William Bak

There is no path to the possibilities
Unless you have mastered imagination,
And are willing to go passed
The boundaries.

This is my take on creation,
To push on evolution.
To beauties and powers
Unseen until now.

> "And what is imagination, but hope?"
> - William Bak

I am a Fox,
With my words,
And imagination.
I am creating dragons,
Dragons of hope.

CHAPTER 41
THE PARROT
MASTER LISTENING

BY DR. BAK NGUYEN & WILLIAM BAK

I am a parrot.
Yes, I repeat what I hear
But I also choose
What I repeat.

Most people think
That because I am a bird,
A have a « bird's brain »
A tiny tiny bird's brain…

I will disappoint you
You'll be surprised
Of all the stupidities
I have to filter
To find words
Worthy of me.

I can fly,

I am smart.
Am I a dragon?

More than you know,
The first rule of a dragon heart
Is to listen carefully.
Even the chickens know that.

Trust me, if there is
A champion in that field,
You are looking at him.

I listen
To understand
The world.

I listen
To comprehend
The people.

I listen
To see the world
For what it really is.

Listening made me smart.
Listening forced me
To filter and to sort out.

I am no King
But I know
All about everyone.

I kept an open mind.
The hardest part
Is to keep an open heart.

When you hear all of what I heard,
The world has so many faces,
So many hidden and ugly faces.
It's hard to keep an open heart
And not to judge.

I deserve recognition
Just for filtering
The world's bad intentions.

It's all about action and reaction.
And then, people wonder
Why is the world such
A dangerous place?

Good press, bad press
There are all words
If you ask me.

"Words are the best friends of lies."
- William Bak

So stop talking with words.
Talk with actions
And with passion!

"The world is what we make of it!"
- William Bak

You'll be surprise
How often the kings and dragons
Come for my counsel.

They are all too busy
To listen carefully
To see everyone
For what they really are.

A bird's brain is what kept
The balance of this world.
Between the good and the least
Between the beautiful
And the none.

I am a parrot
And I do not repeat,
I filter and borrow your words
To show you the goodness
Of yourself.

I hear everyone
And see everything.
Not because I am curious,
But because I have
The skill to do so.
Some will call it
My curse.

I am grateful
For my ability.
I just pity those
Who have no idea
Of who they are
And who surrounds them.

That's why I keep repeating the good,
To help to shape the world into
A better place.

Yes, I dream too.
I can be very patient.
My humility pushes me to accept

My role in the balance of the forces.

I am a parrot
And I am a counsel
To Kings.

Lions and dragons
Both come to me
In need of advice,
From a bird's brain!

> "Size does not matter. Only the size of the heart matters."
> - William Bak

If anything, I learn to never
Underestimate anyone.
Respect everyone
Since their future self
May save you one day.

I am a parrot,
I know people,
I read people.

I am the memory of nature
And by extension,
Of dragons.

CHAPTER 42
WE ARE ALL DRAGONS

BY DR. BAK NGUYEN & WILLIAM BAK

We started this journey a few books ago
Trying to find the way of the dragon.

From a chicken to a lion,
We kept an open mind.
From a lion to a dragon,
We kept an open heart.

Only to understand that this was
Just the beginning.

Dragons can change shapes
So we need to master
The different shapes.

Then, all the other animals

Wanted to become
Dragons too.

A dragon is a Force of Nature.
Dragons are invisible to our eyes.
We went around to understand how
To become a dragon,
And how to change shape,

Only to understand that
Dragons do not exist…

On the other hand,
A dragon heart can be found
In many different individuals.

> "Size does not matter.
> Only the size of the heart does."
> – William Bak

I am a Shark,
A dragon who
Mastered Control.

I am the king of the sea.
I am what I eat

So I must eat differently.
I am a shark,
The shadow of a sea dragon.

I am a Panda,
A dragon who
Mastered Harmony.

I live peacefully with my surroundings,
Aware of not taking more than what I give.
Once in harmony, I can be lazy
I am a dragon of peace.

I am a Rhino,
A dragon who
Mastered Patience.

I can build and destroy.
I prefer to build
With patience, with purpose,
I am a dragon
Because my work will
Live forever.

I am a Hippo,
A dragon who
Mastered Dreams.

I travel the world to stay young.
I am painting the world
With my dreams.

If not mine, then,
Someone else's dreams.
The world is too beautiful and vast
To waste one single day, waiting.

I am a lady,
Not a dragon.
Travelling keeps me
Open and young.

Since I'll stay young forever,
I am a lady dragon.

I am a Monkey,
A dragon who
Mastered Humility.

I am no king,
I don't want the burden.
I am a rockstar!
I am happy
And I make people laugh,
When their heart
Needs to open up.

They all come to me
For a good laugh.
I know who I am,
I am a monkey,
A friend of Dragons.

I fly riding on their back,
The back of dragons.

I am a Pig,
A dragon who
Mastered Gratitude.

I train every day to be better.
I value opportunity and time,
I thank everyone.

Just like lions,
I will outrun everyone
To one day fly as a dragon.
I am a Pig
And I thank you.

I am an Elephant,
A dragon aware
Of his power.

I am a gentle soul.
I do not want to cause any harm
To anyone.
That's why I take my time.

This whole thing
Is about the size of the heart.
Would you like to know mine?

I am no hero,
I am peace and harmony.
I am an Elephant,
A dragon of peace.

I am a Fox,
A dragon who
Mastered Imagination.

I can draw worlds
With my words.
I can make thoughts vivid.
I am writing the legends
Of each dragon.

One day someone will be writing mine,
I am a dragon in the making.

I am a Parrot,
A dragon who
Mastered the art of
Listening.

I hear everything,
The good, the bad
The ugly.

I have to sort and filter all
What I hear.
I see people for what
They really are.

I refuse to let
The bad win.
I repeat the good,
Only the good
To whom might listen.

One day, they will understand.
I am a parrot and I help to make
The world a better place.

I have both the mind
And the heart of a dragon,
Simply because I care.

No matter who you are,
You can find your strengths
And care for others.

That's how your heart will grow,
By sharing.

A dragon is born from the heart.
If you choose so
You can find your heart
And your powers.

We are all dragons!

CHAPTER 43
"A NEW ANCHOR"
by Dr. BAK NGUYEN

I cannot tell how surprised I am travelling this journey. It's been less than a month, and we achieved the unthinkable. You heard me talking about it since the beginning of this book, but trust me, there is more!

Didn't I tell you that we had to leave for New York City right after Christmas? We were supposed to go to the Big Apple to catch a cruise to Florida, Miami to be more precise, and then, go to the Bahamas.

The trip was intentional for William to be on camera and to prepare small video segments to promote our trilogy, his books.

Between the travelling, the checking in and out of hotels and the accumulated fatigue, it was a challenge just to have the energy to go on, leave alone to perform in front of a camera... oh and I forgot, William is 8...

I took us one day to settle in, and by the 27th, we were shooting throughout the beautiful landscapes of New York. I have to tell you that William bore the whole thing on his shoulders, he was ready and motivated.

As soon as we say action, William is a pro!

Of course, he was there when I did a photoshoot with Tranie a few months earlier in Las Vegas to promote her book: **THE POWER BEHIND THE ALPHA**.

He also had numerous occasions to see me performing in front of a camera, particularly in New York, about two months ago, talking about **REBOOT**, my book on Midlife Crisis.
But to see him perform just like he had done that all his life was a magical moment to the whole team! With energy, wisdom, and enthusiasm, he made the shooting fun and productive, more than I had hoped for!

Haven't I told you that my power is **speed** and **momentum**? While everyone wanted me to rest, I was struggling to keep up my pace. Ask a tornado to stand still, and you will have killed it... and died trying.

William gave me a way out! He was such a charm to work with that I started editing his video right away, from my iPhone in the middle of Fifth Avenue, waiting for Tranie to shop.

I edited one, and two, and three videos. With each final video, my morale was boosted to the maximum.

Some of those videos were intended to promote the **Trilogy of the Chicken/Lion/Dragon Heart**. Because it went so well, we made some more about **WE ARE ALL DRAGONS**, the new project that William pushed for.

The 25th, I compiled the structure and the imagery to be ready for **WE ARE ALL DRAGONS**. The 26th, we arrived in NYC at around 3 PM and had to check in and find a place to dine.

After a long drive, we were all exhausted, and some people from my team started to show signs of illness due to a bad contagious cold. The signs weren't so good...

By the 27th, William embraced his role as an author and a leader and brought in his magic on. The 28th in the morning, we checked in to the cruise ship, that took most of the day…

By the 29th, I was feeling a little seasick since I applied my patch against motion sickness just as I arrived on the boat.

I really can't remember when we had the time to write it, but we did. Nine chapters of **WE ARE ALL DRAGONS**, exploring how each animal could reach their dragon heart.

I wrote based on the videos I shot and edited of William. Not just those in New York, but also the one we shot on the ship and in Florida.

I was writing between the lost time and the waiting… waiting for people to be ready, waiting for the excursion, waiting for I don't even know what… I am supposed to be at least, half in vacations and enjoying.

Enjoying I did, very much.

Until then, I had William's words and enthusiasm about how he sees the future and how he wanted part of my endeavors. Now, I have actions and results to show beyond my own expectations.

I've never produced as much, as fast with such ease. New York was a revelation to me, Will-I-am proves his worth as a son and a partner.

The 31st, around noon, we were out of **WE ARE ALL DRAGONS**, twice, in French and in English. The last two hours' sprint allowed us to finish the translation to French and ensure that we would meet our deadline and the world record of 8 children's books within a month.

For Christmas this year, I didn't just give William eight books and a world record, I gave him the **Confidence** that nothing is out of reach, and based on the dragon's myth and ancient Chinese folklore, I gave him **INFINITY**! The infinite of all the power of the dragon: **wealth, wisdom, courage, nobility**...

> "I gave him the endless sense of possibilities."
> Dr. Bak Nguyen

The beauty in the process is that at 8, he understood everything and was actually motivated by the idea of **infinity**! He took in the belief and started to spread his own magic to support the vibe.

The whole team was motivated by our new anchor, William Bak.

The backup plan was to film me, talking about my journey writing 15 books within 15 months. Once again, William stole my thunder... actually, I gladly gave up the *baton* to him. I couldn't be prouder of my son.

By the 31st, we were finished, and celebrating!

Even if we achieved our goal, we did not stop filming. At each location and each day, William recorded one or two videos.

What is truly amazing is that I did not prep him for long, usually, we agreed on a subject, and he just went on and... improvised! I cut and edited and voilà!

> "I thought it was hard, but with my dad, it's easy!"
> William Bak

Those were his words in his first interview talking about writing. I can tell you that I will say the same about him. With William, it was simply a charm, easy and smooth!

I don't know what will follow next. While writing the children's books, I kept writing this one, **THE BOOK OF LEGENDS** on the side to share with you my thoughts and feeling writing with William. This is the last chapter.

I am finishing my thoughts with the sun at my right, shining over the balcony of my room. With the waves rocking me, I feel like living in a dream, writing a legend.

I really wish that the movie will never end. I don't want to be back to an average life. Not this time! Nothing ever felt so real and bright, with hope looking ahead!

"Hope and fear are siblings that can be very similar."
Dr. Bak Nguyen

This time, there is hope and no fear, since William proved his worth. He is asking to join the ranks without any pressure from my part.

Do I need to remind you that I was simply fulfilling a year-old promise?... I know now that whatever is ahead, the **DRAGON'S BOOKS** and the **BOOK OF LEGENDS** will have bonded our imagination and destiny together.

I know that I won't stop. Now I am eager to see what William will do next! Isn't wonderful? Competition without jealousy! Partners without comparison! Whoever will push forward wins!

... a game where there is no loser!

We are all dragons, only if we choose so. Dragons are invisible, they change shape at will, and they do not fight each other. We will oblige by those rules, William and I.

William and I.

May you join us on this wonderful journey.

CONCLUSION
by Dr. BAK NGUYEN

I am a little sad that this adventure is reaching an end, at least partially. William still wants to write more, and I will encourage him to do so.

As for me, I have other projects to return to. I am grateful that within a month, I've discovered a whole new world to fatherhood.

As a year just went by, a new one is starting. The era where Dr. Bak is no more. William is joining the team and will stay on. We are not the Avengers nor the Justice League, we are **Legends and Dragons**.

"Legends and Dragons"
William Bak & Dr. Bak Nguyen

This is our journey, our legacy, our story together. I will let William take over with his views and ideas while I will take the backseat for the following months.

With the achievement of this book, we signed nine books together on a period of one month and three days! To empower others, to help people find their dragon's heart, to make the world a better place, those are our values.

To aim for perfection and not to stop at a **NO**, that is our promise. But more importantly, we need to keep evolving, with an open mind and an open heart.

We are all dragons, so we must unlearn to learn again. Each new shape is the beginning of something new, each new skill is a journey by itself.

I don't know where William will stir **Legends and Dragons**, but in him, I trust. Not just because he is my son, but because he proved his worth and his resilience when it was required of him.

I've worked and collaborated with many people, only a few can match and follow my pace. William has pushed my pace to new heights.

> "What to expect from the unexpected?
> To be able to embrace gracefully."
> Dr. Bak Nguyen

This has been a magical ride in this holiday's season. I am grateful and enjoying every single moment of it, as a parent, as a dad, as bff...

As a parent, we are proud and hopeful, but there is always that downside, where the kid will turn spoiled, out of control to end up wasting a golden opportunity, and to turn it into the biggest failure of all time.

I need to respect William and to give him some credit. I cannot choose from him, I can only prepare him. This is exactly what our books are doing, to prepare and to share, with him, with me, with the other parents and their children.

> "We are all dragons!"
> William Bak

Each of us has to eventually find our name and our identity. Each of us will have the chance to write our own legend if we choose to do so.

Some will do it on their own, some will be rejected by society first before they could find theirs. This journey and this book prove that we don't need to be alone.

William kept me company and gave me hope and empowerment. We saw the **synergy** as we put our minds together and created.

I know that I can't be his soul mate, for that, he will still need to go out and search for that single person dedicated to him. But I have surely shown him how it feels like to be in **symbiosis** with another soul.

> "Without giving, there is no taking.
> That's the spirit of a team."
> Dr. Bak Nguyen

He knows that to grow, he must share and be a man of his word. I am doing my best to live up to the highest standards to inspire him to find his own way, his dragon's shapes.

We flew together, and that was just the beginning.

But let's go back a minute to the danger of the famous child, the spoils that corrupt the genius.

Yesterday, he went swimming with the dolphins with his mom. Our deal is that he keeps on doing two videos a day, talking about **Legends and Dragons**.

He dropped the ball and didn't take his duty seriously. He did record two videos, but almost pointless videos and way too short...

I was upset, but ok, I would respect his choice. He would be fired! Fired from **Legends and Dragons**. Of course, that was just a way for me to see how he would react.

His reaction was surely what I had hoped for, but never could have expected. He embraced his mistake, swallowed his pride and went in front of the camera to talk about his failures...

Nothing too big, but just enough to make him understand that he cannot be part of a team and drop the ball without consequences... on him and the rest of the team.

He recorded one of his best videos ever, with honesty and humility. I was moved as I held the camera, listening to his words.

> "Humility is the acceptance of who we are, truly. This is no pretension since it is the truth."
> Dr. Bak Nguyen

William at 8, was courageous enough to go on camera to take responsibility and to apologize. His involvement with me and our books were bigger to him than his pride. This is a Lion Heart! We all recognize the thread.

If I can keep his attention and trust, William will not be spoiled, since he will be taking responsibility. He will still live with abundance, now that he knows how to create values and abundance. And what good is abundance if not sharing?

I am a good dad, thanks to my son. I am a fulfilled man, thanks to my legacy. I am happy, thanks to William.

When I think of it, do you know that being a father was what scared me the most? I wasn't ready to put someone else's evolution before mine, I still had so much to accomplish.

That was 9 years ago. Today, if there is anything I can say about fatherhood is that fatherhood upgraded all my system.

> "Love and fatherhood fixed and improved most of my systems and core beliefs."
> Dr. Bak Nguyen

Since fatherhood is the ultimate serving exercise, I became a better man, a stronger man, wiser and with the **depth of resilience**.

It's never just about me anymore, but about us. I still have a lifetime in front of me to describe and find out who is **US**!

No, William will not be walking in my footsteps, he will be leaving his own footsteps, next to mine. I always preferred myself as a big brother than a father.

I will not cast a shadow on him. I cannot stop to evolve, and will continue my legend either way. All I can do is to believe in him and encourage him to embrace his walks, his swims, his flights.

At 8, my son is becoming a man faster than his mom and dad wish for. But to Dr. Bak, it is a much anticipated moment to shake hands with the future of our world, William and all the dragon hearts that he will help empower.

It was and still is a true honor to have shared those magical moments with William and with you.

This is my take about parenting, may it help to inspire all the fathers and mothers out there. Your story has just begun.

We are all dragons if we choose to be so.

Dr. Bak Nguyen

EAX

ENHANCED AUDIO EXPERIENCE

A new way to learn and enjoy Audiobooks. Made to be entertaining while keeping the self-educational value of a book, EAX will appeal to both auditive and visual people. EAX is the blockbuster of the Audiobooks.

EAX will cover most of Dr. Bak's books, and is now negotiating to bring more authors and more titles to the EAX concept.

Now streaming on Spotify, Apple Music and available for download on all major music platforms. Give it a try today!

FROM THE SAME AUTHOR
Dr. Bak Nguyen

TITLES AVAILABLE AT
www.DrBakNguyen.com

MAJOR LEAGUES' ACCESS

FACTEUR HUMAIN
LE LEADERSHIP DU SUCCÈS
par DR BAK NGUYEN & CHRISTIAN TRUDEAU

ehappyPedia
THE RISE OF THE UNICORN
BY DR. BAK NGUYEN & DR. JEAN DE SERRES

CHAMPION MINDSET
LEARNING TO WIN
BY DR. BAK NGUYEN & CHRISTOPHE MULUMBA

BRANDING DR.BAK
BALANCING STRATEGY AND EMOTIONS
BY DR. BAK NGUYEN, BRENDA GARCIA & SANTIAGO CHICA

BUSINESS

La Symphonie des Sens
ENTREPREUNARIAT
par DR BAK NGUYEN

Industries Disruptors
BY DR. BAK NGUYEN, ROUBA SAKR AND COLLABORATORS

Changing the World from a dental chair
BY DR. BAK NGUYEN

The Power Behind the Alpha
BY TRANIE VO & DR. BAK NGUYEN

SELFMADE
GRATITUDE AND HUMILITY
BY DR. BAK NGUYEN

CHILDREN'S BOOK
with William Bak

The Trilogy of Legends

THE LEGEND OF THE CHICKEN HEART
BY DR. BAK NGUYEN & WILLIAM BAK

THE LEGEND OF THE LION HEART
BY DR. BAK NGUYEN & WILLIAM BAK

THE LEGEND OF THE DRAGON HEART
BY DR. BAK NGUYEN & WILLIAM BAK

WE ARE ALL DRAGONS
BY DR. BAK NGUYEN & WILLIAM BAK

The Collection of the Chicken

THE 9 SECRETS OF THE SMART CHICKEN
BY DR. BAK NGUYEN & WILLIAM BAK

THE SECRET OF THE FAST CHICKEN
BY DR. BAK NGUYEN & WILLIAM BAK

THE LEGEND OF THE SUPER CHICKEN
BY DR. BAK NGUYEN & WILLIAM BAK

THE STORY OF THE CHICKEN SHIT
BY DR. BAK NGUYEN & WILLIAM BAK

WHY CHICKEN CAN'T DREAM?
BY DR. BAK NGUYEN & WILLIAM BAK

THE STORY OF THE CHICKEN NUGGET
BY DR. BAK NGUYEN & WILLIAM BAK

LEGENDARY

IDENTITY
THE ANTHOLOGY OF QUESTS
BY DR. BAK NGUYEN

HYBRID
THE MODERN QUEST OF IDENTITY
BY DR. BAK NGUYEN

FORCES OF NATURE
FORGING THE CHARACTER OF WINNERS
BY DR. BAK NGUYEN

LIFESTYLE

HORIZON, BUILDING UP THE VISION
VOLUME ONE
BY DR. BAK NGUYEN

HORIZON, ON THE FOOTSTEP OF TITANS
VOLUME TWO
BY DR. BAK NGUYEN

MILLION DOLLAR MINDSET

MOMENTUM TRANSFER
BY DR. BAK NGUYEN & Coach DINO MASSON

LEVERAGE
COMMUNICATION INTO SUCCESS
BY DR. BAK NGUYEN AND COLLABORATORS

THE POWER OF YES
MY 18 MONTHS JOURNEY
BY DR. BAK NGUYEN

HOW TO WRITE A BOOK IN 30 DAYS
BY DR. BAK NGUYEN

POWER
EMOTIONAL INTELLIGENCE
BY DR. BAK NGUYEN

MENTORS
BY DR. BAK NGUYEN

HOW TO NOT FAIL AS A DENTIST
BY DR. BAK NGUYEN

HOW TO WRITE A SUCCESSFUL BUSINESS PLAN
BY DR. BAK NGUYEN & ROUBA SAKR

MASTERMIND, 7 WAYS INTO THE BIG LEAGUE
BY DR. BAK NGUYEN & JONAS DIOP

PARENTING

THE BOOK OF LEGENDS
BY DR. BAK NGUYEN & WILLIAM BAK

THE BOOK OF LEGENDS 2
BY DR. BAK NGUYEN & WILLIAM BAK

PERSONAL GROWTH

REBOOT
MIDLIFE CRISIS
BY DR. BAK NGUYEN

THE ENERGY FORMULA
BY DR. BAK NGUYEN

PHILOSOPHY

LEADERSHIP
PANDORA'S BOX
BY DR. BAK NGUYEN

KRYPTO
TO SAVE THE WORLD
BY DR. BAK NGUYEN & ILYAS BAKOUCH

SOCIETY

PROFESSION HEALTH
THE UNCONVENTIONAL QUEST OF HAPPINESS
BY DR. BAK NGUYEN, DR. MIRJANA SINDOLIC,
DR. ROBERT DURAND AND COLLABORATORS

WHITE COATS
THE UNCONVENTIONAL QUEST OF HAPPINESS
BY DR. BAK NGUYEN AND COLLABORATORS

LE RÊVE CANADIEN
D'IMMIGRANT À MILLIONNAIRE
par DR BAK NGUYEN

TITLES AVAILABLE AT
www.DrBakNguyen.com

www.ingramcontent.com/pod-product-compliance
Lightning Source LLC
Chambersburg PA
CBHW070634160426
43194CB00009B/1461